THE
grace-filled
HOMESTEAD

- - - - - - - - - - - - - -

LANA STENNER

TEN PEAKS PRESS
EUGENE, OR

Scripture quotations are taken from the Holy Bible, New International Version®, NIV®. Copyright © 1973, 1978, 1984, 2011 by Biblica, Inc.® Used by permission of Zondervan. All rights reserved worldwide. www.zondervan.com. The "NIV" and "New International Version" are trademarks registered in the United States Patent and Trademark Office by Biblica, Inc.®

Published in association with literary agent Tawny Johnson of Illuminate Literary Agency, www.illuminateliterary.com.

Cover design by Faceout Studio, Lindy Martin
Interior design by Faceout Studio, Paul Nielsen

Photograph on page 19 by Trisha Wray
Photograph on page 158 by Carl Molle
Photographs on pages 120 and 212 by Makena Hubbs
All other photographs by Lana Stenner

For bulk or special sales, please call 1-800-547-8979.
Email: Customerservice@hhpbooks.com

▲. This logo is a trademark of The Hawkins Children's LLC.
Harvest House Publishers, Inc., is the exclusive licensee of this trademark.

The Grace-Filled Homestead
Copyright © 2022 by Lana Stenner
Published by Ten Peaks Press, an imprint of Harvest House Publishers
Eugene, Oregon 97408

ISBN 978-0-7369-8466-9 (hardcover)
ISBN 978-0-7369-8467-6 (eBook)

Library of Congress Control Number: 2022931419

Printed in China

22 23 24 25 26 27 28 29 30 / RDS-FO / 10 9 8 7 6 5 4 3 2 1

TO MY
PRECIOUS FAMILY
CJ, Colton, Cameron, Isaiah, Sophia, Madalyn, and Riley Rose—

"You Are My Sunshine"

- - - - - - - - - - - - - -

We know that in all things God works for the
good of those who love him, who have been
called according to his purpose.

Romans 8:28

Contents

The Grace-Filled Life

Let us dance in the sun wearing wildflowers
in our hair and grace in our soul.

Susan Polis Schutz

Homesteading is literally in my blood.

I descend from the pioneering spirit of my great-grandparents, who crossed the plains in a covered wagon to stake their ground in Missouri. Many of the flourishing branches of my family tree have lived lives of self-sufficiency and simple beauty. And I am no exception. My parents were both raised on small farms in different states. I loved hearing the stories of chasing escaped baby pigs, using the cold creek water as a natural milk refrigerator, and my Nonnie heading to the coop to select the Sunday dinner chicken. While some kids may have cringed at the rawness or work of it all, I found it exciting. Even magical.

Years went by, cities crowded in, and my grandparents began the transition to city life. By the time I came along, the family home was in an average Midwestern suburban neighborhood. I grew up with all the typical trappings of a '70s and '80s childhood, including roller skating rinks, peach Nehi soda, and fabulous TV sitcoms. For entertainment, I searched for coins in the couch cushions so I could ride my bike to the convenience store and play the Pac-Man video game machine. All these activities were enjoyable, yet by the time my mother hollered for us to come in for dinner, my friends and I had made our way to the woods behind the neighborhood and were catching tadpoles in the creek, jumping on logs, and building forts in trees. The new video games could never compete with the alluring call of the outdoors.

This was my happy place.

My parents kept our homesteading heritage alive in the suburbs in small ways, including the creation of a small garden in the backyard. Some of my fondest memories are of spending time in the strawberry patch with my mom. It was pure delight to pop a juicy berry in my mouth, straight from the plant. The large ones we would buy from the store in off-seasons were nothing compared to the sweet burst of flavor from those tiny homegrown berries that we harvested from our own yard each June.

I hold these memories with such gratitude because those moments collectively got me hooked on gardening at a very young age. And this fascination with gardening became my connection to loving the land and wanting to spend my time honoring and interacting with it. This childhood of digging, planting, and enjoying the fruitfulness of the earth prepared me for the life I would share with my future husband.

I grew up and married my high school sweetheart, CJ, a true outdoorsman. We began dreaming of our future life together in a home surrounded by fields of flowers, vegetable gardens, and lots of room for babies. Our first five years of marriage, however, were a fast-paced blur. After college, I started my career in the corporate financial world with long hours and lots of stress. CJ worked at an intense job for the airlines, but it came with the wonderful benefit of free travel. From the outside, it looked like we were at the beginning of a successful, on-track life. We had a house in the right neighborhood, two incomes, no little ones yet, and weekend trips to the coast or wherever we wanted. But we knew the toll that this "good life" was taking. We worked too hard and too much, striving to be happy. By the way, striving to be happy is not a healthy formula for actual happiness!

Like a lot of people in this stage of life, we soldiered on and managed the fast-paced hustle as exhaustion set in. Then when child number one was born, we recognized that we were both spiritually dry and, honestly, depleted in every way.

We became reinspired by our dream of the simple homestead lifestyle God had laid on our hearts years before.

It was time to follow a different path…the right path for us. With anticipation and an occasional case of nerves, we started planning an exit. We found ways to simplify our careers, home, and spending habits so both of us could enjoy what was more important to us—our growing family. Every month, we took another step toward our homestead lifestyle goals. Within a few years, we had four babies and had greatly reduced our expenses, so I became a stay-at-home mom. And best of all, we moved to a small hobby farm on four acres just inside the city limits.

The Grace-Filled Homestead was born.

We are now approaching 20 years on this property and are still pursuing the art of slow living. We've chased fireflies on warm summer nights, watched our kids push one another on the tire swing, and built a tree house in the old oak tree. We've held a baby goat minutes after it was born, we've gathered fresh eggs from the coop before breakfast, and we still love pulling the first juicy grapes off the vine before the birds devour them.

God, goats, and gardens are a few of our favorite things around here. But the list of blessings grows with every sunrise. I want you to see these, experience them, and gather those that suit your life right now. Sure, maybe someday you will make a bigger leap (maybe you recently did!), but the best news of all is that it doesn't matter. This way of living will serve and nourish you and your family wherever you are. You only need to start. Maybe it will merely be a perspective shift that opens you up to all this goodness, grit, and grace.

I invite you to embrace your own homesteading lifestyle. The heart of this adventure is the pursuit of slow living and growing deep roots in faith, family, and the farm (even if it is from your apartment patio). My hope is to encourage your desire to seek beauty in your surroundings, cultivate bonds with those you love, and work hand in hand with God.

I want to point to the blooms, the goats, and the chicken coop and let you in on some of God's gentle truths that shine in my backyard and in your own spaces—old things can become new again, there is beauty in being different, embracing imperfections is freedom, and so much more. These insights are nourishing no matter where you live. If you've joined me online, you know I also love to share practical insights, my favorite scratch recipes, and surprising facts about the life we've sown, planted, and harvested at the Grace-Filled Homestead.

That's all here in this stroll you and I will take through the joyful homestead life.

If you long for simplicity and authenticity and a change that has seemed elusive, let's make our way to the sunflower-lined path. But first, I'll meet you on the front porch with a glass of peach tea. I'm excited to show you around.

Blessings,
Lana XO

CHAPTER ONE

Slow Living
Chasing Fast Goats

Goats are fast little stinkers, and they chase after their dreams. Whether it's climbing on the lawn furniture to reach the delicious wisteria blooms or sneaking into the neighbor's pasture to frolic and play on a new hay bale, they know what they want, and nothing will stop them from getting it. If there is a sturdy six-foot-tall fence, they will break through the middle of it, dig under it, or even climb over it hoof by furry hoof. And it is quite a sight to watch. These adorable scoundrels are stealthy smart and will team up with their goat gang to distract you with snuggles while a couple of them dash through the gate at warp speed to get to those yummy bushes on the other side. Why can't we be a little more like this when it comes to chasing our dreams?

There is no waiting or indecision with goats. They go for their dreams. They are full of action and adventure and are not afraid to fail and try again. They will continue failing and trying again all day long until they get what they want. The problem with us humans is that we are indecisive and give up too easily. Doubt, pride, and fear of failure keep us stuck every time.

If you have a dream tugging at your soul, I believe you have an obligation to yourself and your Maker to explore it. There is a good chance God gave you that desire and it's a part of his plan for your life.

The Dream of an Unhurried Life

In every state across this country, there is a movement of those dreaming of going back to the basics, growing their own food, and slowing down their pace. Their dream is the homestead movement. They are trading in material possessions for a raised garden bed and a rooster. Individuals and families are saying goodbye to the busy hustle and seeking out a life of intention and purpose. It is less about the amount of space you have and more about the mindset. We are picking back up those old family recipes, cultivating the vegetable gardens, and spending more time on the front porch with those we love.

We began our marriage living in the fast lane. I was speeding in traffic headed to a high-rise financial office downtown in a sea of cement to grind through a 12-hour day. And yet we had a dream of raising our family simply, cultivating that black dirt in the veggie garden and watching barefoot toddlers chase one another in the dew-covered grass. We yearned for God's simple pleasures, like the wild and free children enjoying nature. I envisioned family meals around our table where the kids could ask their grandpa about the Bible and we could discuss current events and devour a scrumptious farm-to-table meal that was made from scratch. This would be a life of intention and moving toward self-sustainability. When we decided to go for it, it didn't make much sense to our friends, but we did it anyway.

Laser focusing on what you want will many times mean leaving some other things behind, and that is hard to do. Especially if what you are leaving behind is also good, like a job, neighborhood, or even a relationship.

Many of us have the desire down in our hearts to be a homesteader and slow down our fast-paced, consumer lifestyles, but we hesitate to have that dream because we don't live on a farm. A farm is not needed to enjoy life's simple pleasures. You can follow your dream in a downtown apartment. Think of those early pioneers living in the backs of covered wagons for months and even years. Slowly, as the wooden wheels turned, making progress over the rocky trail, they were making their way from homelessness to the fulfillment of their dreams of freedom on the open range.

The early pioneers lived a simple life out of necessity, with long days of labor and minimal possessions. They were intrinsically grateful and possessed an appreciation for God, their loved ones, and what little they had. My dream was to get back to those basics.

Sunshine Street

The first time I laid eyes on our mini farm was just over 20 years ago. We were preparing to build a new home on a few acres we had purchased down the road. We were getting out of the neighborhood and would finally have space for a larger garden and chickens. As we were drawing up building blueprints, our neighbors mentioned that a nearby older couple was planning to sell their 100-year-old farmhouse on four acres. We drove down the street to check it out, and bright yellow rays of sunshine were beaming from the corner property. Seriously, the yellow farmhouse was so brilliant, you needed sunglasses to witness the glory.

Instantly, I fell in love with its charm and the idea of raising our babies on a fairy-tale family farm full of history. I had visions of my baby girl with me riding piggyback through the field with the boys running ahead of us. The wild kids were free and climbing the pear trees to pick the juiciest fruit ever known to man. In my "love at first sight" vision, I'm pretty sure the bluebirds were chirping and angels were singing. Oh goodness, it was awful and beautiful all at the same time. I could easily see past all the fixer-upper projects and focus on that huge oak tree that needed a tire swing and giggling toddlers on it.

The owners of the mini family farm were named Herb and Dollie, and they were the most precious couple I'd ever met. They had been married *forever*. They raised their young family in Colorado and eventually made their way to the Kansas City–Liberty, Missouri, border. Herb adored his bride, planting sugar maples for her on Mother's Day and tending to her orchard trees. And as the years progressed and the stairs became too tough for her to climb, he moved their bedroom to the main floor.

You could tell theirs was one of the true and rare love stories. Long before the recent "she shed" trend, Herb built Dollie her own adorable workshop and craft house for her porcelain doll–making kiln. Dollie named it the Carriage House, and it was complete with a bathroom and studio kitchen. Herb and Dollie were in their eighties. Their eyesight and movement were becoming limited, and they were faced with some difficult decisions for their future.

We were in love with that property but found out they already had offers on the table. Oh, I was heartbroken. CJ reached out one last time even though its fate had been sealed. Surprisingly, they invited us over. Dollie knew God's destiny for our clan and insisted on selling their home to the fireman's family with all the sweet kids. We obviously didn't bring the wild kids into the house to meet her. They were playing out front, an acre away where you couldn't hear the name-calling and sibling "you idiot" banter. All rowdy children look precious from an acre away, right?

They picked us. Yes, us...and with that one decision, everything changed. The circa 1900 farmhouse came complete with 1970s light fixtures and the standard worn green shag carpet. Over the past 100 years, there had been several minor additions, with the last remodel in the '70s. That was obvious. The kitchen was tiny, and there were not enough bedrooms for our large family. Without a master bedroom or bath, we moved our bed into the ten-by-ten den and used the bathroom off the kitchen. The boys were excited to share a bunk room, and all of us were thrilled with our new old farmhouse.

Recalculating Directions . . . Where's Easy Street?

Before moving in, we were instantly hit with thousands of dollars in septic, roof, and basement repairs. With me being a stay-at-home mom and a fireman's salary providing for six, times were tight and we were frugal. CJ is handy with tools, so we

did most repairs and updates ourselves. Many critical projects had to be put on the waiting list. "We'll get to it when we get to it," we said.

We also had our share of homestead mishaps, like a huge black snake finding its way into the bathroom, 11 wild baby raccoons being born just above our master bedroom ceiling, and an F3 tornado coming through the back of the property just after dark. Simple living on a small farm sounded so romantic and peaceful. What the heck had we gotten ourselves into? We often wondered if we were even cut out for this lifestyle.

We quickly learned how much hard work was required to live out our dream, but the traditions and joy that come with moving into someone else's family farm are indescribable. They hand you their memories, and you promise to carry on their heritage and family values. Herb and Dollie have both since passed away but have left us with their legacy. At Herb's funeral, we enjoyed hearing stories from their grandkids. My favorite was Dollie sending a grandchild to the airport with freshly made applesauce in a glass too hot to hold. Now that is fresh.

God, Goats, and Gardens

Goats don't give up when the situation gets tough. They find a way to persevere and reach their goals...over, under, or right through that sturdy wire fence. When you are pursuing a dream, the smallest of doubts can threaten to derail your plans. A part of our homestead dream was raising mini Nubian goats. We had a glorious garden and daily chicken eggs from our feisty flock, but we dreamed of silly tiny goats frolicking through our back pasture and, of course, that yummy goat milk cheese.

Just a few years ago, mini Nubians were a rare breed. I found a farm that had three for sale a couple of hours from our home. This family had hit hard times, with the husband in bad shape and preparing for surgery. They no longer could take care of their animals and needed to sell them ASAP. CJ was at the fire station, and I was on my own, so I loaded up the old jeep with two large dog kennels and was off on a new adventure.

The sun was shining on that chilly day, my car radio was tuned to happy music, and I was singing aloud as I knocked out those miles between me and my dream. As I arrived and pulled into their beautiful property, doubt started to creep in as I wondered if I had what it took to raise these little ones. This property had the perfect setup, with multiple barns, pastures, sheds, and ponds. Is there such a thing as fence envy? If so, I had it. They had the ideal setup on sprawling acreage, and we did not.

The Comparison Game Breeds Doubt

Who did I think I was? Our farm was tiny, our barn was an old shack, and our fencing didn't exist. I had ordered an electric fence on Amazon but hadn't put it up yet. What on earth was I thinking? I was not equipped for this. I needed at least two more years to get ready for this undertaking.

The woman was so kind, asking me about our setup. It was clear she loved her goats and wanted them to go to a good home. She then said, "Let's go meet the kids and see if they like you. They are a good judge of character." This family was giving me their precious kids, and I was not worthy to even babysit them for an hour. She pointed at Pistol Pete, a feisty little one jumping from platform to platform in her goat playground. One more thing I didn't have. Sweet Molly was snacking on some hay. When they realized I didn't have a snack for them, they turned away and went back to what they were doing. Well, that was a strike one and two. Hopefully, I wouldn't strike out with number three.

Then we went around the corner to find Gloriann laying up on a platform. Oh my word, she was huge! "Mini" Nubian? She had to weigh 150 pounds. How on earth did she get her large rear end up there? She gracefully jumped down and strolled over to sniff me. She put her big head under my hand as if to tell me to scratch her ears. She took a nibble at my jacket and then would not leave my side. "Oh, she loves you already. Hooray, it's meant to be," the owner said as I was thinking there was no way she was going to fit into that kennel in my car.

The next hour was tough and left me swimming in sweat and a pool of doubt. She suggested that we load up Gloriann first since she was the largest. We proceeded to attempt to pick her up together and were unsuccessful. One…two…three…lift, with her on the front and me on the back. This goat was huge and awkward and all of a sudden felt slippery, although she was dry. We were in the middle of nowhere with no help. I suggested we use the large sheet of wood laying against the barn to make a ramp. That was unsuccessful, as it broke under her weight.

After an hour, we backed up the jeep to a rock pile to attempt to walk the goat up it. It was important that the rocks were sturdy and the path didn't break her ankle. After the first two unsuccessful tries, the owner looked at her watch and asked if I could give her a minute to check on her husband, and she was gone.

She left me there standing with all my doubts and Gloriann nestled up, trying to get her ear scratched again. I was done. I was in way over my head, and it was clear I needed to throw in the towel and go home. Again, what was I thinking? I needed to get out of there…now and without these goats! I could jump in the car and be on the highway before the farmer came back. Just then, she came out of her front door and hollered up at us both, "Don't get discouraged ladies, we will get over this hurdle. You two are meant to be together." She walked up, stepped back to analyze the mound of rocks, and suggested we lead the big mama up a path a few inches over.

The grace-filled life preserves the simplicity, beauty, and dreams of unhurried days.

It worked. Gloriann glided slowly up that mound with her head held high as if she was gracefully walking the red carpet to enter an awards ceremony. Surprisingly, she fit into the kennel. She plopped down comfortably and started chewing her cud like she had been there her whole life. We made quick work of getting the smaller ones in together, and then it was time to leave. As the farmer handed me the paperwork and snack packs filled with sliced apples and celery, she said, "You are going to be a great goat mama." And I was off. A bit nervous but mostly excited and grateful.

If you have that homestead spirit in your soul, when problems seem insurmountable, you will persist and figure it out. Slow living takes a lot of work and determination not to give up when things go south.

Following a dream is not for the faint of heart, and simple living is full of hard work and mud. Oh, but it's worth it. When we wake, there is a beautiful sunrise and pasture full of goats out back. At dusk, we sit on our front porch and watch the sunset over the barn. We've had goats napping in our laps, bonfires, lemonade stands, firework displays, and lots of smoked barbecue. As with any dream, the picture of the struggles is not clear until you are knee-deep in that pile of manure. But I can honestly say, no moment is better than when your boots are muddy and your heart is full.

BOOKSHELF FLOWER BED

Repurposing items is part of a homesteader's DNA. Our herb garden is a raised bed made from an old bookshelf that was wasting away in the barn. This is an easy way to add plants to your garden without building a raised bed. The unexpected bonus is that the shelves become wonderful dividers between plants.

SUPPLIES

— Wooden bookshelf

— Food-grade sealant

— Gravel

— Compost

— Potting soil

DIRECTIONS

1. Place the bookshelf backside down in the desired location.

2. If you're using it for flowers, give it a good cleaning with the garden hose. If you're using it for herbs or edible plants, sand and seal it with a food-grade sealant.

3. Drill 2 small drainage holes between each shelf if there is a back to the bookshelf.

4. Remove the shelves if you want one open bed, or keep them if you prefer dividers.

5. Fill it with a layer of gravel, and then add compost and potting soil.

6. Plant to your heart's content and enjoy!

CINNAMON ROLL COFFEE CAKE

This delicious coffee cake is a family favorite at the Grace-Filled Homestead. Pair it with a strong dark roast coffee to balance the sweet vanilla icing. One bite and you'll be hooked for life.

INGREDIENTS FOR COFFEE CAKE

(Boxed yellow cake mix can be substituted for the first 4 ingredients)
— $2\frac{1}{4}$ cups unbleached all-purpose flour
— $1\frac{1}{2}$ cups sugar
— $3\frac{1}{2}$ tsp. baking powder
— 1 tsp. salt
— 4 eggs
— $\frac{3}{4}$ cup vegetable oil
— 1 cup sour cream
— 1 cup brown sugar
— 1 T. cinnamon

INGREDIENTS FOR ICING

— $\frac{1}{4}$ cup milk
— 3 cups powdered sugar
— 1 T. vanilla
— 2 T. butter

DIRECTIONS FOR COFFEE CAKE

Mix the flour, sugar, baking powder, and salt. Then add the eggs, oil, and sour cream. Pour the batter into a 9 x 13-inch greased pan. Combine the brown sugar and cinnamon. Spread the mixture on top of the cake, and with a butter knife, swirl it into the top of the batter. Bake at 325° for 35 to 40 minutes and then let it cool.

DIRECTIONS FOR ICING

Mix the icing ingredients in a separate bowl and add it to the top of the cake. Serve it with strong black percolated coffee. Enjoy!

CHAPTER TWO

The Feisty Flock

Bringing home baby chicks is a rite of passage for homesteaders.

The first time I held the fluffy, yellow babies on our return from the feed store, I had pastoral visions of sweet hens free ranging in a field of flowers and my kiddos skipping out to the coop to gather colorful, fresh eggs each morning before breakfast.

In the homesteader-honeymoon daydream, I couldn't imagine the mountains of chicken poop and squawking attitude that come with raising a feisty flock. Our chickens have a double dose of sassiness. Over the past 15 years, we have learned so much about these creatures.

As the desire for organic food and sustainable living grows beyond the limits of rural farms, backyard chicken coops are popping up all over urban neighborhoods. Many municipalities now allow their community members to experience a little bit of farm life within city limits, although city dwellers have restrictions on how many and who they can have in their coop. Roosters are commonly banned because those stinkers can be extremely loud for neighbors who may not appreciate our feathered friends the way we do. An unwelcome five a.m. *cock-a-doodle-do* just might get you kicked out of the Friday night neighborhood bunco group!

I'll share more about him later, but it's safe to say that our rebellious bully of a rooster would get us ousted from any civilized community.

Even though we started off naive, it became clear in only a few months that embarking on a homestead life would be a great adventure. An outdoor school of sorts with a curriculum of learning as we go, knowing only enough to be dangerous, surviving a hodgepodge of personalities, and discovering grace in the chaos. What more could a girl born into a legacy of homesteading want?

Have a Purpose and a Plan

As with anything on the homestead, knowing your purpose and planning ahead when raising chickens will keep the chaos to a minimum. The purpose of our chickens is pure enjoyment and, of course, the abundance of eggs. We are in this adventure for the food and the fun. Although we do not process our birds for meat, we do have several homestead friends who do. Of course, you'll need to determine your purpose for raising a flock before you let your kiddos become best friends with their pet chickens. You don't want them to become that 35-year-old adult lying on a therapist's couch, blaming you for eating their best friend.

We've been raising chickens for over 15 years and started with a handful of chicks before we even had a coop. It was a bit backward, but we made quick work of getting them set up. I wonder how many naive families come home from the farm feed store with a few adorable Easter chicks that were not planned for. They are so cute and irresistible at that age, but then reality hits and you find yourself hustling to find shelter for them when you get home.

Most homesteaders purchase their day-old chicks from a local feed store. We have also ordered baby chicks online from a hatchery hundreds of miles away. I was skeptical about ordering chicks online, but they arrived in a small crate from the post office, happy and healthy.

One season, we allowed nature to take its course—we stopped gathering the eggs and encouraged a brooding hen to sit on them. We carefully watched her as she nested, fluffed her bedding, and rarely left her warm eggs. Within a month, they hatched, and soon the little chicks made a trail behind her. This mother hen was a good mama. Although it's not the most efficient process and requires some separation from other chickens, it was fun for our kids to experience the joy of natural hatching.

This past spring, we hatched a set of chicks from an incubator. We kept the incubator box in the kitchen, and the entire family was enamored with the whole process. We found ourselves anxiously sitting around the box, waiting for them to hatch.

One thing we didn't plan for was that our barn-kitty-turned-diva, Princess Easter, would become keeper of the babies. She decided to spend the entire 21 days lying on top of the incubator. At first, we thought she was waiting for a snack, but that didn't fit her character. Frankly, she's a bit of a food snob. Unlike most cats, she would never think of sneaking into the trash or killing something. She expects her food to be served in a silver bowl, and we, as her servants, comply with her request. We wondered if Easter just liked the warmth of the incubator for her napping spot, since it's kept at a pleasant 100 degrees. However, when it was time to open the top to see the first chick hatch, Easter raised up purring and couldn't wait to snuggle up to the little yellow furry ball.

It takes about 21 days for the sweet fluff balls to poke their way out of the shells and into our world. Their next stop is the brooder, which is their home for the first couple of weeks. We keep them warm and cozy under the heat lamp with access to fresh water and chick crumbles.

It never gets old to see new life emerge right before our eyes and to witness the surprise responses from the rest of the animal kingdom. Who knew her royal highness, Easter, had the heart of a mama? And even though we dreamed of this existence, we could not have planned or prepared for the adventure of falling madly in love with each new life entrusted to our care.

A RAINBOW OF EGGS

Most baby chicks will lay their first egg within five months of hatching, with or without a rooster. I chuckle every time I think of a hen being a true feminist. Each breed is beautifully unique, with different egg colors and personalities. Typically, hens lay either the light-brown or white eggs, but the rainbow of hues can be stunning. The blue of the Ameraucana, the deep brown of the Marans, and the greens of the Olive Egger are a few of our favorites. They are all delicious in a morning scramble covered in cheese.

The Coops . . . and the Poop

The care and feeding of our brood changed as we learned more about what works well, what gets us by, and what might be a big miss. You don't always know which you're investing time into. Thankfully, coops for the adult birds are easy to build, and there are many different options and styles to provide critical shelter from predators. We've had sneaky coyotes, raccoons, and even a fox scouting out the pen. Our first coop was an old deck box originally used for lawn furniture cushions. It wasn't pretty, but it was functional. We enjoyed this simple setup until we built the ladies their palace.

Because we were expanding the flock, we needed more room for the sassy hens to spread out. We scored a free children's playset on Craigslist and combined it with the coop we already had. It took us a couple of weeks to complete it, but it

was pure joy to watch the girls strut around in their beautiful home addition for the very first time.

And of course, what's a diva coop without a chandelier? Although the fixture is very fancy, it also has the important function of keeping the chickens laying through the winter months. Our region regularly sees subzero temps and snowstorms, so the heat bulb helps cut the chill.

Chickens are fairly simple to keep. They require plenty of clean water, access to chicken feed, and some bedding of straw or pine shavings. Foraging for bugs, scratching through grain, and eating leftover berries are their favorite forms of entertainment. For a special treat, they get leftover salad greens, or I make them a scrumptious ice cake filled with fruit during the warm summer months.

Then there is the less desirable aspect of care. Who wants to clean the coop? No one! Well, except the goats. They love coop-cleanout day because they are allowed to join us in the forbidden playhouse and take rides in the wheelbarrow. For the hardworking humans, it is a different story. The mountain of poop I mentioned earlier does not seem like an exaggeration when you're cleaning it up. Jot this down as another truth about this adventure: With the bad comes the good. And so it goes that with the poop comes goodness. Those piles produce a wheelbarrow full of compost gold for our garden beds.

After we deep clean the coop, we love to spray it down with a DIY essential oil spray to keep the mites and infestations away. It smells heavenly and can also be used in a teenage boy's room. I'm not sure which smells worse, a boy's bedroom or a chicken coop.

Personalities, Pecking Orders, and Poetry

Although chickens can be kept in a small area of your backyard, you will find that they quickly take up the full space in your heart. Most people don't realize

that chickens make wonderful pets. They each have different personalities and can be very friendly, especially if they are handled often when they are young. My sidekick, Daisy, would affectionately join me every day as I completed my garden chores and then proceed to nap in my lap in the afternoon sun.

I've noticed throughout the years that observing the dynamics of the flock can often reveal character traits that we can recognize in our own lives. When free ranging, the hens are sweet and mind their own business, but in the evening, when they are in tight quarters inside the coop, a pecking order surfaces (which is where we get the term) and irritation levels rise. One of our hens, named Lucy, was especially picked on. Little Daisy, the sweetest and sassiest of the hens, made it her duty to diffuse situations and protect the weak. She would position herself right in the middle of the group of ladies and squawk if one of them attempted to peck at her bestie, Lucy. Observing the ladies can be a lesson in kindness, compassion, and grace.

And then there's Britches.

If you have followed the escapades of the Grace-Filled Homestead, there is a good chance you might have heard the folklore surrounding our infamous rooster. Britches had quickly become famous in our neck of the woods and even had his own painted portrait hanging on our dining room wall. He just happened to be our very first rooster after he somehow sneaked into the hatchery's bin of female day-old chicks. It took us a couple of weeks to realize that one of these chicks was not like the others. Although it's great to have one rooster to protect the flock, roosters are not needed for the hens to produce eggs. We have since added that to the list of things we learned after we already had chickens.

As a baby chick, Britches was adorable and sweet, but his disposition turned south as he became the savage protector of his harem. Songs have been written and stories told about mean roosters, but I had no idea the depth of their truth. Britches was a bully to all humans, but he had a special place in his dark heart for *me*. My children often told me that he could sense my fear, which apparently made me his number one target. He would lurk nearby like a predator waiting for a moment of weakness in their prey. My young son Cameron was taking Spanish at the time and appropriately nicknamed him Diablo, or Satan in Spanish.

At 20 pounds of solid muscle and with sharp talons that glistened like swords, Britches would listen intently for the tires of my car coming up the gravel drive. Next, he would sprint to the front of the property to harass me before I even had a chance to open the car door. All too often, I would sit in the driver's seat, gathering my wits and courage, before making a mad dash into the house. A play-by-play strategy quickly developed in my mind as I planned how I was going to survive the ambush. It was then that I would remember what I was wearing. *Oh goodness, why am I in shorts and flip-flops when I should be in full body armor? Ready…set…go!*

As I flung the car door open, I blocked my calves with the bulky grocery bags and started running as fast as I could. First to the right, then quickly to the left, in a deliberate zigzag motion to throw him off. Every day I needed to come up with a new game plan to keep him on his talons. Wouldn't it be nice to have an attached garage that I could pull into so I wouldn't have to deal with him? Friends and family did not believe our stories until they too found themselves sprinting for their lives across the yard to avoid his unrelenting wrath.

Britches loved to catch you off guard. If I was bent down working in the garden, he would quietly sneak up behind me, jump high in the air, and ninja kick me over with both feet. As I face-planted in the dirt, he would dart away to safety at warp speed. He knew his life was in danger for the 60 seconds after an altercation. It usually took me that long to gather my senses, my self-control, and whatever was left of my dignity.

I vowed that this could not go on any longer.

As I recall, it was an ordinary Tuesday. The sun sat up high in a clear blue, Missouri sky, and butterflies darted in the breeze. In this tranquil setting, over the last couple of months, the random attacks had become a daily occurrence. Tension around the farmyard was running high and reached a tipping point on that unsuspecting day. It seemed Britches was wanting to claim new territory. And it was all going down on the homestead.

The main event was to be played out in the strawberry patch and promised to be pay-per-view worthy. A slight breeze ruffled the kale and carrot tops in the garden, and the property fell deathly quiet.

I sensed his presence mere seconds before he attacked me from his favorite vantage point—the rear. But at that moment, before my face took a dive into the dirt, slow-motion-like, I vowed I was not going to go down without a fight. What followed mimicked a UFC match, complete with screams and smack talk. CJ, my fireman husband, rushed out of the house and, like a referee, began pulling us apart. Luckily for me, he had gotten off shift and just happened to be home. There was no way I was going to tap out no matter how badly my opponent tore me up. When it was all over, we staggered to opposite ends of the property, my neck gashed and his beak bloody and battered.

That was it. I had had enough. Just as a middle school girl plots how she'll stand up to her mean bully, I took the entire afternoon to plan out my strategy of how to keep him from terrorizing anyone ever again. That evening, as Britches held his chest out and herded his ladies back into the coop, we had a moment. Eye to eye.

As the latch came down, locking him into his final prison, he stared deep into my soul and gave me what I thought was an ever so slight nod. He knew he had crossed the line and probably wasn't going to be allowed back out again any time soon. He was now locked in the coop run, never to free range again. Winner, winner, chicken dinner. Speaking of which, our friends and family made jokes about

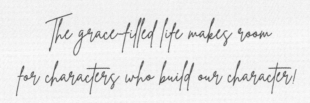

The grace-filled life makes room for characters who build our character!

turning him into a pot pie. I, however, committed myself to taking the high road and was glad for what I considered to be a win-win situation.

My bully was locked up, but he could live. By my kindness and unmerited grace toward Britches, he was allowed to keep breathing. I call it kindness with boundaries.

Scripture is filled with passages about extending grace to others that don't deserve it. Our answer just happened to mirror some wisdom gleaned from the poetry of Robert Frost: "Good fences make good neighbors."

So I extended grace freely to Britches—from the other side of a very strong wire fence.

Poetic justice for the win.

READY YOUR ROOST

(Be sure to consult your municipality for any restrictions on keeping hens or roosters in your area.)

Adding chickens to your property can be fairly easy and affordable. Most farmers start their baby chicks in a smaller box called a brooder and then move them to the larger coop after a couple of weeks. When introducing the chicks to their new home, carefully dip their beaks in the water and then the food so they know where the nutrients are located. Keep new chicks warm with a heat lamp set at 95 degrees. Each week, you can gradually reduce the heat by 5 degrees. Add fresh water, food, and clean bedding daily.

Here are a few simple supplies needed to start your homestead flock—urban or rural:

— Chicken feeder
— Starter feed
— Water container
— Pine shavings bedding
— Brooder box
— Coop shelter with a nesting box
— Roost or branch
— Heat lamp
— Baby chicks

Get ready to fall in love with your sassy feathered friends and enjoy delicious fresh eggs daily within six months.

COOP OIL SPRAY AND SATCHEL

Essential oils are a wonderful way to sanitize the coop after it has been cleaned, and a fresh rosemary herb satchel is the final touch when cleaning our nesting boxes. Rosemary is an insect repellant and deodorizer and helps with chicken respiratory health. The refreshing scents instantly turn the coop into the hens' happy place.

SUPPLIES
— Lemon essential oil
— Rosemary essential oil
— Peppermint essential oil
— Glass spray bottle
— 5 sprigs fresh rosemary
— Small muslin bag or 6 inches of twine

SPRAY DIRECTIONS
1. Add 5 to 10 drops of each oil to the bottle.

2. Fill the rest of the bottle with water.

3. Shake and spray on every surface.

SATCHEL DIRECTIONS
1. Add fresh sprigs of rosemary to the small hanging muslin bag or tie the small herb sprigs together in a bundle with twine.

2. Place it in the nesting box.

We prefer to tie the herbs with twine, as it allows the ladies to nibble on them. Chickens will enjoy rosemary as a snack (your teenage boys won't).

EGG AND GRUYÈRE FRITTATA

This easy egg frittata recipe has just a few simple ingredients. Fancy folks call it a frittata, but around here, we call it egg crud. It's a delicious start to your day and makes a fabulous main dish for a simple brunch in the garden.

INGREDIENTS

— 1 T. butter
— 1 cup yellow onion, chopped
— 3 cups baby spinach
— 2 cups smoked ham, cubed
— 1 cup heavy cream
— 8 large eggs
— 2 cups Gruyère cheese, grated (Swiss can be substituted)
— Salt and pepper to taste

DIRECTIONS

Preheat the oven to 350°.

Melt the butter in a skillet. Sauté the onions for a few minutes until transparent. In the last 30 seconds, add the baby spinach to soften it. Remove from the heat and add the ham. Distribute the ingredients evenly into a greased 9-inch round dish.

In a separate bowl, whisk together the cream, eggs, and $1\frac{1}{2}$ cups of cheese. Season with salt and pepper. Pour the egg mixture over the top of the onion, spinach, and ham. Sprinkle the remaining grated cheese on top and bake the frittata for 35 minutes. Avoid overcooking so it isn't dry. The frittata is done when an inserted knife comes out clean.

Serve with fruit, hot sauce, sour cream, or whatever will make a dreamy breakfast.

CHAPTER THREE

Goats, Giggles, and God

Goats are pure happiness.

You can't help but giggle when around a goat because silliness permeates their DNA. Our family has concluded that goats are the best animal God has gifted the world. We feel so strongly about this that it becomes a bit irritating to walk through stores and see llamas and sloths on T-shirts and mugs, but never a baby goat. The world just doesn't know what it's missing. In recent years, the term "GOAT"—Greatest of All Time—has become a trendy phrase, so maybe there is hope for humanity.

Goats really are the Greatest of All Time.

Our herd of mini Nubian goats is full of mischief and bliss. One minute they're jumping on the lawn furniture to nibble a wisteria bloom or breaking through the fence to the neighbor's pasture, and the next moment they're wanting to snuggle and either leaping into your lap or nudging your leg until you give them some love. When curiosity gets the better of them, goats will sneak into the back door of your house and all the way into your heart. Most goat owners gladly admit that once they experienced the joy of goats, they were hooked for life.

I just know that after your time with our goats today, you will be too. Their joy has filled our lives, and now it overflows from every story I tell—whether it's about how to spoil them, how to keep up with their merry-making, or how our little runt overcame his obstacles with love, hard work, and perseverance.

The Good Goat Life

Goats don't need much to live their healthy, happy lives: fresh water, lots of hay, and a safe shelter. We spoil ours with a daily scoop of yummy herd feed filled with grains, bird seed, and minerals specific to their needs. Occasionally, there are goat shots and a spa pedicure for hoofs, but their upkeep is less complicated than that of our farm dogs—Rosie the redbone hound and Elsa the Great Pyrenees mix are the true high maintenance divas of the property.

Don't let the "mini" in mini Nubian fool you. This goat breed can often get well over 100 pounds! They are absolutely adorable with their long droopy ears, snuggly personalities, and amazing milk. We've milked our goats in the past, but we don't do it every day like many goat farms do. We go through seasons with our milking and get as much as we can just after the baby goats are weaned. Nubian goat milk is desirable because it has the highest fat content of any breed. Those beautiful girls can produce a gallon of milk per day, which is wonderful for making soap and my favorite cheese.

Goats like to relax in the afternoon—much like humans. After grazing on greenery and bushes all morning, they will find a comfy spot in the pen to plop down and chew their cud. Cud is partially digested forage, regurgitated from one of their stomach chambers for a final chew…gross, I know. Once that is swallowed, it moves on to the next chamber of the stomach for further digestion. After they chew their cud, it is siesta time. Goats love to nap. Most of the herd gets up with the sun and then likes to recharge and relax a bit later in the afternoon. Except

for Honeynut. She likes to sleep in and is grumpy toward those rowdy goats who have too much morning energy. She gets her burst of ornery energy about the time the others want to relax in the afternoon, and then it's payback time for Honeynut.

How do you keep adventurous goats in the pen? You don't. Goat fencing is unbelievably important, and of course, we learned that the hard way. We've had goats go under, break through, and climb over the fence to get to their buddy or an irresistible leafy bush on the other side. We recommend five-foot-tall fencing at a minimum. And you should splurge on the durable options—trust me, it's worth the expense. The good thing about our goats is that strangely enough, they are homebodies. Once they break through to the other side, they usually stay within a few feet of their home pen. They are all about the adventure but not necessarily the destination. If only we could all be a bit more like that.

Comical Coconspirators

Joining in on the herd's mischief and silliness are William and Harry, our English Southdown babydoll sheep. Their breed is often referred to as smiling sheep. They are best buds with the goat gang and always follow the goats' lead. Sometimes, I wonder if they think they are goats! If Lily the goat jumps off a tall mound of dirt with a side kick, they all take turns and mimic her moves, including the sheep. Sheep typically graze on the low grass while goats snack on shrubs, branches, and foliage higher off the ground. Lately, we've been watching the sheep raise up on their hind legs and eat the leaves off the trees just like the goats do. It's a cute sight to see their pudgy little bodies standing up. They just want to be a part of the cool-kids goat gang.

But when this band of rascals joins forces, it's unbelievable how much trouble they can get into. They act like a group of bored teenagers looking for some fun. They have taught one another how to climb over a fence and even open a gate latch. They also enjoy sneaking into the berry patch for treats, busting into the chicken coop to hear the ladies squawk, and—as in their most recent misadventure—breaking into the hay storage.

One afternoon, I discovered the entire herd was not in their pen, and I became frantic. I kept calling their names while covering the entire acreage repeatedly. My last stop was inside the winter hay storage barn, which was an unlikely hiding place because it was secured by a shut door. As I twisted the handle and shoved the door open, I heard a sweet little *baaa* coming from what seemed to be high up and toward the back of the barn. No way could they have gotten into the forbidden hay storage—it required someone to turn a doorknob! But they did.

"Someone" somehow turned the knob and made sure the door was shut behind them so I wouldn't find them in the middle of their mischief. When I walked in, I soon located the bandits on top of their mountain of contraband—bales of delicious hay. There they were, two sheep and eight goats bloated and sprawled out on their sides. Sleepily, they lifted their heads to tell me they were glad to see me. Having eaten more than their bellies could possibly handle, they were miserable. They looked like I feel at 3:00 p.m. on Thanksgiving, having eaten two different family meals. These scoundrels seemed thrilled and grateful to be rescued from their own misguided adventure and happy to be shown the way back home.

This merry band of hay-thieving goats makes me chuckle daily, just like I thought they would. What I didn't expect was for one little goat guy to steal my heart...and make it even more tender toward the Lord.

His name is Totes MaGoats. And his story is a good one.

A Mama's Heart and the Father's Love

It was one frigid Midwestern evening in February when the temperature was well below 20 degrees, and shimmering icicles hung from the barn roof. The barn

windows were beautifully frosted over in the corners, and sunlight cast a honey glow across the floor. But there was someone in pain who didn't care about the picturesque scene. Gloriann, the oldest in our herd, was pregnant and uncomfortable and wanted to have that baby now! We are a small farm without all the high-tech gadgets and sonogram tools, so we had no idea how many babies she would have. We all were hoping for twins to double the fun.

As Gloriann continued to shift positions, we knew the time was near. The poor mama-to-be could not get comfortable. After 20 hours of active labor, Gloriann gave birth to three kids, one baby girl and two boys. Little Lily and Gus came out bleating loudly, letting everyone at the farm know they had arrived. Their delivery was smooth and uneventful. That is just how you want it. Their due date was Valentine's Day, but the sweethearts made their debut a day early!

But Totes was different. In more ways than one.

Totes was the tiny, precious brown surprise who came minutes after the other two were born. We never dreamed we would welcome triplets! Although some of the other goat breeds have up to four or five babies at a time, it's usually one or two for Nubians. This third little buckling was all curled up and barely breathing. And he was ice cold. Gloriann had her hooves full attempting to clean up the healthy two. We knew it would be up to us to help him survive the night. He was wet, covered in afterbirth, and too weak to cry. A silent newborn goat is the first indication of distress. He did, however, open his gorgeous brown eyes, bat his long eyelashes, and look right into my eyes. It was all over for me in that moment. I had a mama's heart for this little guy. Apparently, my husband was pretty smitten too.

CJ suggested that we bring him in the house to warm him up by the fire…God bless that man. It was freezing outside in the barn, and this darling baby was not moving. We grabbed a couple of towels, I scooped him up in my arms, and we made our way into the house. CJ wiped him down with more clean towels to dry

him off, and I nestled him right up by the fire. We set up our own little NICU in our family room to regulate his temperature. Since the baby was unable to feed from his mother, we prepared to bottle feed him. As we held him, he would look up at us with beloved brown eyes that melted all our hearts.

It was clear that he was in a tight spot in his mama's belly, because his neck and ears were misshaped. We also discovered that the little trooper's back leg was limp and would be unable to support his weight. We began massaging his leg and neck to encourage movement. After 24 hours, he was able to hold his head high and stand on his own for a couple of seconds. Who needs that fourth leg when you can wobble on only three? It was quite a sight for us to watch him push up on his front legs and then bring the one strong back leg up underneath himself. He was determined and getting stronger by the hour.

We soon prepared him a bed in a storage bin and placed it in our bathroom. This is where he earned his nickname "Totes"—from the green plastic tote container that doubled for his bed. Every day, while Totes recovered, we took him outside to the goat pen to hang out with his family. We would carry him out and place him in the straw up against his mama. Lily and Gus would sniff their smaller brother, nuzzle noses, and then jump around and play. Because he wasn't able to move all four legs together, Totes tired quickly and would plop down next to his mama for a quick nap. Our worries that Gloriann would reject him because he spent so much time in the house were put to rest the moment we watched her lick and snuggle up to her little one. The bond between mama and child is very strong—even for goats.

When we eventually made a trip to the goat vet, she informed us that there was no apparent injury or permanent damage to Totes's leg. We were told that he may even get some feeling back. So every evening after dinner, we committed ourselves to giving Totes his physical therapy in order to build up his leg muscles. I would hold his favorite stuffed bunny and run to the other side of the house in hopes that he would follow me, putting weight on his weak leg. We would do stretches and exercises. After Totes's PT appointment, we would wrap him up in a warm blanket, sit on the couch as a family, and watch a Western show on Netflix. He loved every minute of it—and so did we.

Most days, his limp back leg dragged behind him. It was the same size as his other three legs, covered in soft fur with the cutest hoof you ever saw, but it simply couldn't stand the weight. Totes had so many challenges and was so different from his siblings, Lily and Gus. But he was determined to keep up with them. In the days to come, we increased the intensity and length of our PT sessions, and Totes made huge progress. Within two weeks, he was using the leg regularly, eating great, and growing even stronger.

When the spring temperatures warmed up and it was time to send him out to live in the pen with the herd, I didn't want to let him go. In all honesty, I kept him in a few days longer than I needed to because I enjoyed the giggles and fun he brought to the house. As I tucked him in bed that first evening in the barn, it was heartbreaking. As I cuddled that sweet angel, I was reminded of how hard it must be for God, who loves us so deeply, to willingly let us go—to let us forge our own way knowing our shortcomings and our limitations. I knew Totes would be getting into all sorts of mischief with his goat gang. I also knew that when he would break through the fence, raid the hay barn, or crash the chick party in the coop, I'd be there to save him from his own silly self.

Why? Because I loved that little goat.

As I gently laid him down next to his mama and siblings, he snuggled in tight, but not before he popped back up to nuzzle my neck and gaze into my eyes. He was letting me know, with his big brown eyes, that he was a big boy now.

Within two months, Totes rose to be the leader of the pack. Somehow his time in the house made him the cool kid on the block, and he was now running and jumping on all fours, completely healed up. Still, he'll always be our sweet baby. He has reminded me of my own limitations, my own misguided decisions, my own silliness. And my own need for a Savior who loves me through lots of second chances.

My years on the farm have helped me comprehend God's all-encompassing love. It is so much more than we can imagine. While I run through acres looking for my lost goats that have gotten themselves into trouble *again*, God does so much more for us when we've managed to go rogue on a misguided adventure. He seeks us out, untangles us from the mess we've made, and guides us back to his grace-filled path.

God wants to wash off our dirt and mess, wrap us in a warm blanket, and sit for a while on the couch with his precious child. What joy it is to snuggle in tight. Safe. Loved. And in God's presence. It's the best. Actually…it's the GOAT!

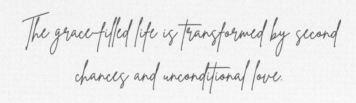

The grace-filled life is transformed by second chances and unconditional love.

GOAT YOGA BASICS

Follow the goat, follow the joy! This saying led us to fall for goat yoga at the homestead. We call it our holy yoga, complete with a Christian worship playlist. Give it a try in your area or on your farm. It can also be done with kitties and pups.

Here are tips for your first goat yoga session:

1. Put your hair in a ponytail or bun so the goat doesn't think it's hay and start to eat it.

2. Wear old workout clothes. You may go home with a hole from nibbling or a manure smear. No worries, it will wash out.

3. Goats can get a nervous stomach when exposed to loud noises, so do your laughing and chatting with your bestie before class begins.

4. Don't expect an intense workout. You will slowly make your way through a handful of the standard yoga poses and Pilates stretches such as plank, tree, cat-cow, warrior, and mountain pose.

While your session will be similar to a standard yoga class, be prepared for snuggles, play, and an endorphin-popping time. It's pure joy!

ICE CAKES TO KEEP THE KIDS COOL

Summer can be scorching hot here on the homestead, and we've found a way to keep our barnyard friends cool on a hot summer's day. The goats love a berry ice cake. It's easy to make, and your chickens and pups will love it just as much as the goat gang does.

SUPPLIES
2 cups berries, herbs, and additional fruit (feel free to leave the peels on citrus)
3-5 cups water
Cake pan (9-inch round or 9 x 13-inch)

DIRECTIONS
1. Fill a round or rectangle cake pan ¾ full of cold water.

2. Add your favorite animal-friendly berries, herbs, or purchased treats to the water.

3. Freeze it for 3 to 4 hours.

4. Run warm water over the top to pop out the ice cake.

Serve it to your backyard or barnyard friends. It's very entertaining to watch them dig in.

DELICIOUS GOAT CHEESE

I am a self-proclaimed cheese addict and am thrilled that making goat cheese is surprisingly simple. Goat cheese has an earthy, tangy flavor and is wonderful for baking sweet cheesecake, mixing in savory dips, or snacking on simply as is.

INGREDIENTS

— 4 cups goat milk, fresh from the barn or grocery store
— $\frac{1}{3}$ cup lemon juice
— Salt to taste

DIRECTIONS

Stirring frequently, heat the goat milk slowly in a pan until it reaches 190° on your digital thermometer. Remove from heat and stir in the lemon juice. Allow it to sit at room temperature for 20 minutes.

Line a colander with 3 layers of fine cheesecloth. Pour or ladle the curdled milk into the cheesecloth and allow it to drain. Carefully gather the ends of the cheesecloth and tie it over a wooden spoon, allowing it to drain into a bowl for 1 hour at room temperature. This allows the whey to drip out. This recipe produces about 12 ounces of cheese.

Stir in salt to taste. Form the cheese into a wheel, cylinder, or your favorite cheese mold. Chill it in the refrigerator in a sealed container for 3 hours. Sprinkle fresh herbs or drizzle honey on the top before serving with crusty bread or your favorite crackers. Our absolute favorite is to wrap a small frozen slice of goat cheese in bacon, fry it in a skillet, and add it to our salads. Delicious!

CHAPTER FOUR

Pruning and Feeling Peachy

Growing fruit produces a life of juicy goodness. And growing in God's goodness produces fruit in a life. It's a glorious full circle vested in planting and harvesting season after season.

After many years on the homestead, I've realized with great delight that the way we care for our plants often mirrors the way God nurtures our lives. The effort and preparation are done for the same reason…to produce fruit and beauty.

On our homestead, we grow pears, apples, and peaches. We also have a small vineyard of grapes, which require similar tending. The way we prepare the ground and then later prune back growth that could hinder the trees' health impacts the bounty we receive from the earth. Both on the homestead and on our journey as people, we don't get the fruit of a good life until we have strong roots and are open to the pruning that is necessary. Harvest season is always worth it!

Growing Deep Roots

First comes the planting. There are many benefits to planting fruit trees in your backyard. They provide great beauty and produce the juicy joy of delicious fruit. And at the start of every season, there is nothing like the sweet anticipation of early fragrant blossoms and late-summer bounty.

Let me share about a favorite of mine—the peach tree. We even named one of our precious little goats Peaches. Her coloring is the beautiful tone of her namesake fruit, and she is the quiet type. Ironically, all the animals love to snack on the golden fruit except for Peaches. That's a stubborn goat for ya!

Most backyard peach trees are purchased from a nursery or a reputable farm. The best time to plant one is in the late winter. In order for peach trees to resist disease and pests, they need to be in full sun for at least eight hours a day. Plant them 15 feet apart unless they are a smaller dwarf variety, which can be 10 feet apart.

It's fairly easy to plant a peach tree. First, dig a hole a few inches deeper and three times wider than the pot the tree came in. Before removing the tree from the container, water thoroughly and gently pull it, holding low near the trunk. Mound up two inches of soil in the middle of the hole and place the root crown in the center. Fill the hole with soil and then water it in.

The key to success is having enough sun and water to strengthen the root ball before the next winter. You can add an organic fruit-tree fertilizer to the ground under your tree branch diameter in the early spring. This same method can work for most other fruit trees as well.

Cross-pollination is needed for some plants to bear fruit. Most peach varieties are self-pollinating. If you have a variety that is not, you can plant an additional tree within 50 feet or graft two varieties onto one plant. Peach trees are surprisingly easy to grow from a dry seed, even indoors on the windowsill. They grow quickly and can bear fruit in as little as three years.

Pruning for Possibilities

Caring for fruit trees is fairly simple and low maintenance. In order to enjoy an abundant harvest in your orchard, though, you do have to face the painful process of pruning. I firmly believe it's more painful for the farmer than the tree because it seems so counterintuitive to cut off living branches and buds.

Some farmers prune their peach trees in the fall after the crop season. We wait for late winter. It's important to remove any broken or diseased branches as soon as you notice them and cut off any little sucker stems near the ground.

What needs to go won't necessarily be a large branch. It may be a tiny, beautiful bloom that has to be removed in the spring. If you have too much of a good thing, you will not bear abundant, healthy fruit. Pinching off many of the promising, tiny fruit blooms is needed to focus the plant's energy for targeted growth.

Just as homesteaders prune their orchards before the season begins, our loving heavenly Father can prune us for a bumper crop to come. As a nerdy plant lady, I often chuckle to myself and wonder what my plants would say if they could talk. "You watered the goat gang before me? Enough already. I'm thirsty!" Or would they say, "Seriously? You are coming at me with dull pruning shears? This is painful!" The latter is how I've talked to God when I'm going through a season of being pared down, pulled back, and prepared.

Pruning is uncomfortable. Humbling even. But it's necessary to experience the growth God has planned. Just when you think you are done with the cuts, it's time to go deeper to get rid of the unnecessary things that hinder abundant growth.

Recently, I experienced a very unexpected season of personal pruning. It came via a terrifying health diagnosis right in the middle of writing this chapter. How interesting is that? I've never been more grateful for my deep, strong roots of faith. They helped me endure the potential fears of the spiritual shears God used to pare away misplaced priorities and literal unwanted growth so I could become whole and healthy.

Seeing Stars and the Face of Jesus

My favorite seasons, spring and summer, were filled with debilitating headaches that pierced my head like daggers when I leaned over to pluck a strawberry or cucumber. When the pain worsened, I finally made my way into the doctor's office in late fall. My to-do list was a mile long and packed with grading exams for the university, doing farm chores, and preparing for the holidays. It was crunch time, and I didn't feel I could take Excedrin and go lie in a dark quiet room again and again.

During the office visit, my doctor suggested a brain scan because the pain I described was different from headaches caused by allergies, migraines, hormones, or a virus. Two days before Thanksgiving, I had a CT scan, was immediately sent for an MRI, and then was told I had a big brain tumor.

It was the size of a large peach.

The neurosurgeon pointed out a section of the tumor that he felt was too risky to remove, but he was hopeful the growth was benign. He wanted to schedule surgery within the week. We sought a second opinion from another top neurosurgeon in the region. The diagnosis was the same. Though for good measure, he added that the tumor was "gigantic." Great. Now that word was in my head too. When I got home, I sat down at the desk where I'd been writing about pruning fruit trees. Dozens of photos of beautiful peaches lay in front of me. I kept looking at them, trying to picture one inside my brain.

The surgery to prune away this unwanted tumor was scheduled for the week of Christmas. As we prepared for this adventure, God's peace fell hard. I've never felt his presence like I did the weeks before surgery. It was as if the air around my family was spiritually charged. All the unimportant tasks and concerns were pruned away. I wrapped up Christmas shopping, taught my final two lessons at the university, and spent as much time as possible in prayer with my family.

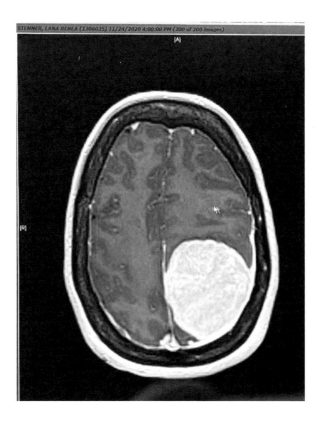

After I removed daily tasks that no longer mattered, I began spending more time out in the barn with the goats. One afternoon, I decided to drag out our large plastic nativity scene that had been in storage for years. It was filthy, janky, and over 20 years old, but I wanted to hang out with my goats and baby Jesus in the barn. The chilly and stinky stall was my happy place where I could meet with God. The goats were snuggly and so silly, always knocking over poor plastic Joseph. They were quick to headbutt anything that came between them and baby Jesus. A lesson for all of us.

While hanging with the goats and Jesus, I had the urge to tell the neurosurgeon to get the entire tumor out. For the love…just get it all! I wanted to explain that our

family members are risk-takers, I'm tight with Jesus, and if everything goes south, it's all good. I'm ready to go to heaven. I decided I would plead my case to take the risk when he came in on surgery morning.

A few days prior to surgery, my bestie sent me a link to an article about the Christmas Star created when Jupiter and Saturn align and appear as one bright star. It's a rare occurrence, and the next one was to happen on December 21, 2020, my surgery day. The article speculated it may have also occurred just as Christ was born, and a similar alignment could have formed the star that led the wise men to baby Jesus. I wasn't in the mood to go down the rabbit hole of researching dates. I'm always a skeptic, so I closed the article and didn't give it more thought.

On surgery day, I arrived at the hospital in the early morning wearing my favorite T-shirt, which reads, "Not Today, Satan." As soon as I signed in, they whisked me to the pre-op area. I didn't even get a chance to say goodbye to CJ. Pandemic protocols meant he couldn't be with me.

Once the IVs were in, I was stripped of my wedding ring and phone, which had my happy worship playlist and Bible reading app. It was just me—raw and alone with God in a chilly, sterile room for the next hour. However, I couldn't feel his presence. The peace I had the past month was gone. For some reason, fear had taken over, and I was full of despair. I cut my baby teeth on the church pew, so there were hundreds of Scriptures I had memorized over the years. And yet I couldn't recall even one to calm my spirit.

I prayed for God to help me get it together.

Suddenly, a 20-year-old worship song came to mind. Three lines of the chorus played in my head over and over. Soon I was humming and singing them to myself and asking God—begging God—to show me his glory, send down his presence, and let me see his face. I felt the calm permeate my soul as I sang these three phrases from the song. I still marvel that all the memorized Scriptures and positive phrases eluded me, but an old Third Day song emerged with crystal clarity and soothed my anxious soul.

The clock on the wall read 7:55 when the nurse popped in one more time to ask if my neurosurgeon had stopped by. Once he did that, I would be rolled to the operating room. It was clear she thought he would have been by for my 8:00 a.m. surgery. Where the heck was he? This was not something you want to turn over to the on-duty intern. Did my surgeon get sick, have a car wreck, decide to retire? I started to spiral again.

The song lyrics came back to me, and so did the calm. Once again, I was begging God to show me his glory, send down his presence, and let me see his face.

Just then, my neurosurgeon pulled back the curtain to my cubicle. He had a clipboard of paperwork in his hand and was dressed in a suit and tie. Really? *Where the heck are your scrubs?* I thought to myself. *Let's get this thing rolling.*

That's when I noticed it. A star on the top of his tie. I remembered the article from my friend and thought, *Good grief, my neurosurgeon is an astronomy nerd.* As he handed the paperwork to his assistant, I got a glimpse of his full tie.

My neurosurgeon was wearing a nativity tie in a secular hospital, politically correct or not. It was complete with the shining bright star, Virgin Mary, Joseph, barnyard animals, and sweet baby Jesus. This was my barn scene at home where I had spent days in prayer, and there was the glorious face of Christ. Just what I had asked for in song during the last hour.

Instantly, I was covered in goose bumps and in awe of the sign God gave me that he was with me. It was such a small detail that meant the world to me in that moment. I was speechless and couldn't form my plea to the neurosurgeon to remove the risky part of the tumor. God was in control and would take care of it all. I was clearly in his hands now.

Four and a half hours later, I woke up.

The grace-filled life bears fruit when we know what to let go of and what to let grow.

I was still alive, so there's that. Slowly, I moved my arms, fingers, legs, and toes…all were working. Thank you, Jesus. I asked for my husband, and they said he couldn't wait to see me. *Wait*, I thought, *I'm talking!* What a relief it was to form a sentence. CJ came in with his eyes shimmering (but of course, the tough fire chief wasn't tearing up), and he told me they had removed the entire tumor. Even though I never formed the words to express my request to take the risk, my heart's desire and prayer were fulfilled.

Later I learned there had been serious complications removing that risky part, and they came out during the surgery to tell CJ that I was bleeding profusely and would need a transfusion. They also told him to expect paralysis. Neither happened. Within hours, I was up walking around and asking about the kids. I felt no pain, even with the 40 staples in my head. I didn't even need Tylenol. They confirmed there was no cancer, there were no deficits, and I was able to go home right away. The bonus…they didn't shave my head.

I was home on December 23, just in time for the holiday joy. The family arrived for a brunch feast on Christmas morning and then again on New Year's Eve. What a miracle to be able to cook, function, and enjoy my family.

Pruning for Possibilities

As the surgeon used his scalpel to remove the tumor, God used his precise tools to prune my heart. This experience cleared distractions and adjusted my priorities so I could flourish in his plan.

Successful pruning requires an expert with a different vantage point to see what is required for maximum growth. A peach tree can't prune itself. Of course, dead branches and leaves can fall to the ground, but healthy abundance occurs after the farmer carefully steps back from the tree, contemplates what needs to go, and then says, "I'm sorry honey, this one is going to hurt, but you will have an enormous juicy peach later this summer if we can get rid of this deterrent life sucker now."

Proudly, I thought I had pruned myself of things that were distractions and dead weight. The homestead life inspires an evaluation of what is most important and certainly what is and isn't worth the use of time and resources. Years ago, I gave up fancy purses, new cars, and numerous other material things. Honestly, driving a rusty old Jeep loaded with a muddy flat of plants from the nursery or a cute goat bleating in the back isn't a sacrifice. Paring down expensive and unnecessary things is freeing, but God is more interested in what's going on in your heart and in your brain…sometimes literally! And the freedom he wants us to have is expansive and life changing, inside and out.

God is involved in all the intimate details of your life. Lean into that truth today. Next season, when it's time to prune my peach trees, I will laugh when I whisper the words of Jesus from John 13:7 to my precious tree: "You do not realize now what I am doing, but later you will understand."

I'm pretty sure I'll follow that with a big amen!

PEACH TREE PRUNING

We prune our peach trees in late winter to encourage health and growth. It is so hard to cut off healthy branches, but trust that it will bring a bigger harvest.

SUPPLIES
— Hand shears, lopper shears, or a pruning saw
— Protective leather gloves
— Stable ladder or step stool

DIRECTIONS
1. Use hand shears for branches smaller than 1 inch in diameter. Lopper shears or a pruning saw work well for larger branches. Be sure your tools are sanitized and sharp before you start.
2. Make needed cuts just above the buds, preferably at an angle.
3. Prune so the lowest branch is at least 15 inches from the ground.
4. Prune to create an open center in the tree to allow for proper sunlight and spacing.

We use an old method to prune peaches that was passed down from avid gardeners. The "cat toss" method suggests that the branches on your tree should be wide enough apart that a cat can be tossed between them without hitting a branch. Of course, our kitties wouldn't approve of this method, so we just eyeball it for our measurements. I do get a little chuckle thinking about this each year at pruning time.

PEACH SWEET TEA

For generations, peach tea has been the classic front porch drink. It's so refreshing on a warm day after working on the homestead. The sweet flavor comes from the fresh ripe peaches.

INGREDIENTS

— 3 ripe peaches, thinly sliced
— 1 cup cold water
— 1 cup sugar
— 4 cups boiling water
— 4 tea bags

DIRECTIONS

Add the peaches, cold water, and sugar to a pan. Bring to a boil, and then stir and simmer for 20 minutes once the peach skins start to fall off. Put a fine sieve over a bowl and pour in the peach mixture. Using a wooden spoon, smash down the peaches into a pulp so as much juice as possible goes through the sieve into the bowl. You will be left with delicious peach simple syrup. Discard the pulp left in the sieve or save it for a delicious smoothie.

Let the tea bags steep in boiling water for 10 minutes. Remove the tea bags and allow it to cool. Add peach simple syrup to taste.

Pour your sweet peach tea into a glass of ice and garnish with a peach slice or sprig of mint.

CHAPTER FIVE

The Land of Milk and Sweet Bee Honey

Homestead living cultivates an appreciation for the joy, provision, and blessings that flow from a simpler way of being. We feel so fortunate to raise our family surrounded by God's creation so they can gather lessons from every season.

On the first warm day of spring, it's a gift to witness the busy activity just outside the beehive. Thousands of tiny yellow flying creatures take flight as if they are warming up their wings for a dance in the sun's rays. The following month, it's enchanting to watch the bees work together to gather pollen on our pink and purple blooms knowing they will return to the hive to produce scrumptious sweet bee honey.

Season after season, we get front-row seats to God's intricate systems and miraculous processes of interdependence within nature and between people. Abundance emerges from all that he has created.

Life in nature with our Creator is meant to be beautiful, shared with others, and sweet as honey. Sadly, I have found that it's easier to focus on the stings of everyday life that occasionally occur than the astonishing moments that are happening around us every hour of every day, like a bee gathering nectar from a flower to make honey. We should be in awe when we behold the simple wonders of God's creation. Let's agree to make it a priority to find that childlike wonder and joy again. The bee apiary is the perfect place to start.

Abuzz with Blessings from the Apiary

"Apiary" is a fancy term that simply means the location of a beehive community. Our humble apiary consists of five hives on the south side of our small property. Other homesteads have hundreds of hives in their apiaries. The larger the apiary, the sweeter the blessings…and probably the more stings. But when you see your child's beaming face after that first finger full of sticky, yummy honey, you know it was all worth it to get that liquid gold.

There is no need to feel left out if you live in an apartment or neighborhood that doesn't allow you to have a beehive. Many local farmers will welcome you onto their property. In exchange for a few jars of honey, they'll let you set your hives on the edge of their field, and in turn, their crops will flourish with the busy bees pollinating nearby plants. Now that is community at its finest, a win-win for everyone involved.

Our family has been keeping bees for many years and has had quite the adventure. Once CJ was driving home after picking up a swarm hive he caught, and the box lid opened when his tires hit a bump in the road. The car was swarming with bees, and yet he was never stung. It took hours to clear it out after he arrived home. I wish we had a video of him speeding into the drive and jumping out of the car.

Every year, we learn more about these fascinating creatures and find new benefits to welcoming them to the homestead. Bees have improved the pollination of our gardens, resulting in more plentiful blooms and a massive veggie harvest. We usually have a few stings each season, but it's so worth it.

Save the Bees and Save the Honey

Bees are moody little creatures. If they don't like their accommodations, they will simply pack up the entire kingdom and leave. They are also naturalists at heart. Of course, most beekeepers know that bees' cute little bodies have no tolerance for pesticides, so they forbid chemicals on their farms. However, you can't control what the farmer down the lane is putting on his crops. The world has taken great strides over the last decade to ensure the health of the bee population, but much is left to be done.

We are doing our part, keeping our small homestead organic and planting the bees' favorite flowers. The cause is near and dear to our hearts, but for us, honestly, it's all about the honey. Just keeping it real.

Honey is considered a superfood. In the homeopathic community and beyond, honey is revered for its properties. It's a healthy alternative to refined sugar and can be full of nutrients like niacin, riboflavin, iron, and manganese. Some say eating local honey can help build up an immunity to allergies. The theory is that because bees are gathering pollen from area plants, when you eat the honey, you consume small amounts of that local pollen and become immunized, lowering the amount of irritation you'll feel during allergy season.

Many nutritionists, grandmas, and homestead hippies alike claim that honey has antibacterial properties, can soothe a sore throat, and can improve your overall health. Don't even get them started about the benefits of royal jelly and propolis. They will talk your ear off. Of course, all health claims should be researched and reviewed with your doctors.

Local bee honey is delicious. The honey found on most supermarket shelves comes from China or South America and has been pasteurized. The heat treatment destroys many of the nutrients, so local fresh honey is always best. The type of flowers that bees collect from impacts the flavor and color of the final product. The most common kinds of honey are made with flavors of alfalfa, clover, or wildflowers. By keeping your own bees and having them harvest from the flowers in your local area, you may end up with a one-of-a-kind honey. It's fun to do a taste test with freshly harvested honey next to one from across town and your jar from last year. Forget the trendy brewery beer flights—a honey flight tasting on your own patio is where it's at. The flavors are always a bit different. Be sure to smear the winner on a warm biscuit, dripping with sweet joy.

The Wonder of a Colony

Honeybees are known as hard workers, but they're also social creatures. They teach us about successful community and hard work. A hive of bees has a complex social structure, their own way of communicating, and many other intriguing aspects that are valuable to learn by observation. The bees in a hive have different roles and work together to feed one another, stay healthy, and reproduce. They are hard workers and take their jobs extremely seriously. Each individual bee diligently works to take care of the colony at large.

Each hive in the apiary is considered its own community and has three different types of bees: a queen, worker bees, and drones. To ensure the health of their colony, they communicate with one another through sound and even a type of hormone. Most of the bees in the hive are female. Bees know how to adapt their environment inside the hive in extreme temperatures to ensure their survival, and most hives will have close to 100,000 bees all working in harmony. Well, that is unless the worker bees are kicking the drones out of the hive for being lazy. No honey for you, slacker.

We've all probably been assigned a school group project or been on a team at work with someone who didn't pull their weight. I can think of one instance from my corporate days. How refreshing would it have been to be like the worker bee

standing at the door, not letting the lazy drone in to get the sweet reward of my work? The worker bees have it all figured out, don't they? They understand the importance of hard work and making awkward, tough decisions for the good of the community.

The worker bees are the smallest in the bee family yet are the most numerous. In addition to gathering the nectar and making honey, they secrete the wax used to make the honeycomb. They also care for the queen and babies and defend the hive against intruders. I consider them the ultimate multitaskers. They also have stingers that will send you away crying like a baby.

The drones are the male honeybees. The only function of a drone is to fertilize a young queen bee. The drones are known as the laziest bees in the colony and only have one thing on their mind—finding a lady to mate with. They don't help take care of larvae, produce wax, collect nectar, or make honey. They feed themselves directly from the honey cells or beg for food from the workers. Such interesting facts that always make me giggle a bit. Nope, I'm not going there.

The queen bee is larger than the others and has the important role of reproduction and laying eggs—as many at 2,000 each day. Goodness, poor thing. If a queen dies unexpectedly or becomes unproductive, she can be replaced. The other bees in the hive will feed royal jelly to one larva so it can mature into the next queen bee. Each kind of bee has a role critical to the survival and health of the colony.

Pillar of the Community

Like the bees, building a community among people takes effort, intention, and care. And we all know creating connections involves hard work at times, especially when establishing different roles to guide the way to the good life.

Perhaps the most important aspect of a human community is interdependence. Just like the bees, we all have a valuable role in a healthy society. This played out in a special relationship with a neighbor of ours. It all began with dropping off a loaf of freshly baked cornbread and honey butter at the doorstep of the older couple across the lane. Like the bees collecting nectar, the simplest of gestures can result in helping others feel cared for as a larger part of a community.

Over the past 20 years, our families and other neighbors have become friends and have formed a tiny community in our neck of the woods. We've joked about how our husbands would try to outdo one another by shoveling the snow off the driveways before the others could get to it. I find it interesting how you venture into a task or relationship thinking you are helping another person out, and then somehow you are blessed by them. These neighbors have blessed our family in more ways than we can count.

On the Receiving End of Sweetness

For years, we were the ones pouring into other families in our community. Taking meals to new mothers, assisting the sick with house chores, and serving hours at our local nonprofits were a standard part of our family DNA. Then one day, the tables turned. When your family member is diagnosed with a serious health condition, you learn the true value of community.

In the days after my peach-sized brain tumor was found, my closest friends rallied like never before. Calls, texts, cards, flowers, and baskets of my favorite things started showing up. Many of these ladies were childhood friends that knew my favorite candle scents, the type of PJ bottoms I liked, and my secret snack of Swiss cake rolls (put them in the freezer before you indulge…you're welcome). There is nothing like the feeling of being known and cared for intimately.

Our large extended family is a community within itself and has always had a deep trust in God's miraculous healing. I decided not to share my health journey with friends and followers on social media. I tried to and just couldn't do it. It felt

spiritually charged and sacred for some reason. However, during that terrifying time, my family added me to every prayer list from one coast to the other and even across the pond. Talk about expanding the community. Prayers were being sent up around the clock, and God was listening to their pleas. How could I be upset about that? My family and their prayer warrior community were sending food, encouraging notes, and scriptures with the promise of a future.

What a year we had! Within a few months of my surgery and full recovery, CJ's dad, Gramps, passed away. Many of those close to us knew he had courageously fought a 25-year battle with cancer. Once again, our community stood with us during a difficult time. My mother-in-love's high school friends began planning food, childcare, and emotional support for all of us. Those ladies had us laughing through our tears at stories of Gramps's mischief back in their school days.

On the morning of the funeral, we were an emotional mess. The funeral director gave the family time in the chapel alone before they opened it to the public. As we opened the doors before the service, we found fire trucks surrounding the drive and a long line of uniformed community servants at the door. Most of these firefighters never met Gramps but were there supporting CJ and our three firefighter sons. Those men and women have a strong tradition of community and live it out daily. These seemingly simple gestures over the past year of trials will never be forgotten, and we are beyond grateful for the love and support of our community.

Dr. Albert Einstein occasionally wrote about widening our circle of compassion beyond a few people to include all creatures and nature. The brilliant Einstein was known to have a fascination with honeybees, their colonies, and pollination. At first glance, this concept of widening our circle of compassion seemed a bit overly sentimental to a gritty gal like me, and yet it is full of truth that I keep coming back to. Widening your circle of compassion is a lovely image for community and embracing others.

The grace-filled life celebrates community, hard work, and God's sweet abundance.

Providing a sense of belonging, doing one's part, and helping others in the community are characteristics found daily in the bee apiary as well as in our suburban neighborhoods, the urban downtown, and small rural villages. What matters more than the money in your bank account, time spent on lavish trips, or worldly possessions is finding the sweet beauty in relationships and caring for others in your neck of the woods, just like the bees do.

THE GIFT OF VANILLA-INFUSED HONEY

Brighten someone's day with a jar of delicious liquid gold! Who wouldn't want a gift of sunshine and sweetness?

Simply add two whole vanilla beans to a mason jar filled with your homestead honey. Create a handmade gift tag and attach it to the jar or lid with twine. Add a handwritten Scripture to encourage a friend or a congratulatory note to honor a special occasion, as we did for a baby shower. You can create a personalized label for the jar. I've brought a jar along with flowers to a hospital visit, to a housewarming party, and as an addition to a girlfriend's birthday gift.

Want to *bee* extra creative? Honey can be infused with fruit, herbs, espresso, and edible flowers, as well as many other things. Just remember not to heat the honey in the process, because it will change the composition. Also, after mixing in your desired infusion, let the jar sit for a week in a cool, dark location before gifting.

BEESWAX KITCHEN WRAPS

Beeswax kitchen wraps are a reusable and biodegradable alternative to plastic wrap, and they are just plain fun with all the print options to choose from. We use them to cover dishes and to store sandwiches, cheese, fruits, and veggies. Don't spend $20 online for a package of three when you can make your own.

SUPPLIES
— 100 percent cotton fabric
— Beeswax from a rinsed comb or craft store natural pellets
— Parchment paper

DIRECTIONS
1. Select, wash, and cut the fabric to the desired size.
2. Lay it flat on a pan lined with parchment paper.
3. Melt the beeswax.
4. Brush the melted wax on one side of the fabric and let it cool.
5. Use the warmth of your hands to wrap an item. Once it cools, a seal is created.

To clean, handwash your wrap in cool water with mild dish soap and air dry.

SCRATCH BUTTERMILK BISCUITS WITH BLACKBERRY HONEY BUTTER

This flaky biscuit recipe has only 6 ingredients and is very simple. Served with the blackberry honey butter, these will take breakfast, lunch, or dinner to the next level.

INGREDIENTS FOR BISCUITS

— 1 cup (2 sticks) unsalted butter, frozen and cubed
— 4 cups all-purpose flour, plus more for rollout surface
— 4 tsp. baking powder
— 1 tsp. salt
— 1 cup cold buttermilk, plus 3 T.
— 2 T. unsalted butter, melted

INGREDIENTS FOR BLACKBERRY HONEY BUTTER

1 cup (2 sticks) butter, softened
$\frac{1}{4}$ cup honey
$\frac{1}{2}$ cup powdered sugar
$\frac{1}{4}$ cup blackberries

DIRECTIONS FOR BUTTERMILK BISCUITS

Place your butter in the freezer for 20 minutes before starting, and then cube into $\frac{1}{2}$-inch squares. This ensures light and flaky biscuits. Preheat the oven to 375° and line a baking sheet with parchment paper. In a large bowl, combine the flour, baking powder, and salt. Use a pastry cutter or a fork to incorporate the butter into the flour mixture, leaving big chunks. Add the buttermilk and stir until combined without overworking the dough. Add a tiny splash of buttermilk if the dough is too dry.

Flour your countertop and roll the dough to $1\frac{1}{2}$ inch thick. Using a 2-inch biscuit cutter or mason jar glass rim, cut the dough into rounds. Place the biscuits on the baking sheet so they are touching. Bake for 17 to 19 minutes. Immediately brush the biscuits with melted butter and serve warm.

DIRECTIONS FOR BLACKBERRY HONEY BUTTER

Whip the butter, honey, and powdered sugar until fluffy. Fold in the blackberries. Mix only until the berries break up and are distributed. Serve in a small dish.

CHAPTER SIX

Dance to Your Own Beet

Just as a painter anticipates their masterpiece even before pouring the paint, gardeners envision the variety of colors, tastes, and textures that will eventually burst forth even while the seeds remain hidden. I purposely fill my garden with an abundant palette of vegetables, berries, herbs, and flowers. Vibrant dahlia blooms happily reside next to the earthy potatoes. Allowing room for variety in our garden cornucopias helps us celebrate the joy and beauty of differences.

You can tell a lot about a person as you walk through their natural spaces. One of my friends has raised beds with perfectly spaced vegetables, mulched walkways, no weeds in sight, and a timed irrigation system. It's well planned out and efficient. Another friend is a carefree old soul with random wildflowers growing with the weeds and fruit vines rambling up the fence. She enjoys tending each plant individually with her watering can. We get to decide what type of gardeners we are and can change our mind season to season.

Embracing Uniqueness in Nature

The garden is a wonderful place to express *your* creativity. At our homestead, we stray far from the typical garden blueprint. The purpose of our garden is pure joy of the senses. The robust taste of the spicy peppers, the deep colors of the root vegetables, the aroma of the blooms, and the feel of the black dirt between my fingers can be magical. We do what we want. Every year it looks different, which keeps it fresh and new. My family doesn't like eggplant, so we stopped growing it. I love strawberries, so we added another patch. It's important to make your garden unique to you. Choose the plants that bring you happiness and reflect who you are.

The best garden layout leaves room for you. Incorporating hobbies and the things that make you happy into your garden space will bring you even more amusement. If you love to read, add a bench in the strawberry patch so you can lose yourself in the pages. A picnic table is a wonderful addition to a garden because you can break bread with those you love while enjoying the fresh produce.

The garden, whether big or small, is your unique masterpiece. Don't wait for Sunday to communicate with God. The brilliant colors in your garden are more beautiful than a stained-glass sanctuary. Here, you can commune with your Creator during the week. Leave room to dance, sway that precious baby to sleep, or enjoy the love of your life under the stars.

Last but not least, pass this creativity, uniqueness, and love for nature to your littles. We have a new baby in the family, so we are building a play space into our garden to give her a plot to dig, imagine, and capture a love for growing at a young age. Let's cultivate the joy of nature in our children.

WILDFLOWERS IN LITTLE HANDS

Muddy hands pick morning wildflowers

Bare feet and skinned knees chase butterflies

Tire swings push toward the sky

Daydreams of castles, kingdoms, and flying to the clouds

Climbing trees and building forts

Frogs in their fingers and mischief in their eyes

Mess makers crafting a masterpiece

"Tag, you're it" ends with giggles and a wrestling match

Outside voices in a chorus of joy

Mason jar fireflies set free

Mud-stained water in the bathtub

Washing adventures away

Precious prayers at bedtime

Grateful to God for a happy day

Planting Memories

So many of my childhood memories revolve around unique and interesting plants. I remember heading outside to play as a little toddler while wearing my favorite dress with frills and a bow. I had a laid-back, cool mom who let me wear what I wanted, mismatch my colors, and change multiple times a day. She encouraged my creativity and uniqueness.

That particular day, I pulled off my shoes and socks and left them in a pile on the porch. The warm spring grass tickled underfoot, and I was a wild child running free in our yard. Suddenly, I stopped in my tracks when I came upon our towering snowball bush. It had been blooming for more than a week, but that day the floral scent was the essence of a fairy tale. As the wind picked up and swirled against the house, it rustled the aged snowball blooms, and the tiny white petals showered all around me like a storm of magnificent snowflakes. It was magical, and I felt the pure peace and joy that only God and his nature can bring. I have since added a snowball bush to our property so I can experience the enchantment of that day again and again.

Honor your stories and draw inspiration from your favorite childhood memories in nature. The scents, shades, and shapes of plants that come to mind could be just what is missing from your yard, your garden, or your acreage.

Perennial Petals and Edible Blooms

Homesteaders as a whole are practical and full of grit. They often skimp on flower gardens and creativity out of necessity. Of course, filling the canning cellar with veggies for the winter months is much more important than tending to flower blooms. Who has time to waste when the cucumbers need to be planted, the sourdough batter needs tending, and the chickens need more scratch grains? However,

I've got good news: Perennials and edible flowers are the answer to the practical homesteader's dilemma.

I love perennials, especially Shasta daisies and echinacea coneflowers. At the garden center, you will notice the distinction tag on seeds and plants declaring annual or perennial. Perennials are God's gift to a busy gardener. Once you plant them, they will come back more abundant every single year. Hooray for beautiful blooms with little work!

I consider annual flowers to be like that vibrant and fun high-maintenance friend. They bring you so much joy, but you are exhausted after you're with them. You can only handle a couple of these relationships. Likewise, every garden needs a few very special high-maintenance annuals, but these are more work, so choose wisely. I love my zinnias and dahlias, but they need to be replanted in my zone every spring. It's a good thing they are beautiful and worth it!

Edible flowers are another option for that practical gardener who doesn't have the resources to tend plants that are only for looks. These blooms are beautiful, practical, and delicious. A few of my favorite edible flowers are pansies, violas, chamomile, lavender, calendula, roses, dandelions, and peonies.

I use edible flowers in teas, flatbreads, fruit popsicles, pastries, and more. A cake topped with violas or peonies is absolutely gorgeous and delectable. We have devoted an entire raised garden bed to our edible flowers. Celebrate these easy-growing flowers in your garden. Do a little dance, ponder God's artistry, and take in the joy of these edible and beautiful blooms.

Veggies as Fuel

The homesteader community often gets a bad rap for being so unique, different, and borderline weird. I will admit that there were a couple of years in particular that we fit that label. Fuel prices were high, and we owned an old diesel SUV. CJ had an idea that he was researching—to convert our engine to run on used vegetable oil. YouTube was new at the time, and there were only a couple of videos on the subject, but we thought, *Why not give it a try?* Famous last words.

Oh, how our kids hated it. The filtering system took over their play space in the barn, and it was a sight to behold. It looked like a huge moonshine distillery with barrels, tubes, and filter socks hanging from the rafters. Not to mention the smell of French fries and fried fish that permeated the air for 100 feet around the car as I picked the kids up in the car lane at school. The children didn't get a say in this adventure, but the money we saved allowed us to take them on a few trips. One of which we will never forget.

The mountain vacation to Colorado was memorable, but not in a good way. The engine blew up and died on the trip down from Pike's Peak. We knew oxygen intake was important in the fuel systems of a diesel engine, but we didn't realize just how little oxygen was waiting for us at the 14,000-foot altitude of the Rocky Mountains. Oh so much fun it was on a road trip with four young kids...true memories were made that day. Needless to say, the car was towed, we rented a minivan for the trip home, and we got a new engine. We eventually sold the veggie-fueled car and filter system to a family in Texas, with clear instructions to keep it out of the mountains.

When you are unique and trying new things, you are forging your own path. Difficulties come up, things break, and plants wilt. It may not be easy, but it is worth it. New experiences and strange adventures will allow you to lead a full and fabulous life that is uniquely yours.

Be an Original

In fourth grade I was 9 years old, going on 16. I made a new friend who had recently moved to our area, and she was the cool kid in class. Forget being authentic and

original, I wanted to be just like her—clothes, hair, and attitude to boot. We were trouble together, and that was new for me. In the spring of that year, I remember getting excited in the days leading up to Arbor Day. Our school gave out trees to each of the fourth graders to take home, plant, and nurture. I was already a plant nerd, but most kids in class never knew I had a fascination with moss growing under trees and wild mushrooms. It was my little secret.

This was the year I would get my own tree. A birch with shimmering leaves and white bark. How cool was that? We'd been studying the great state of Missouri and its native plants and trees, and I couldn't wait to get my tree in the dirt. I had the perfect spot in the rock garden out back, and my parents were on board.

The morning we were to get our trees at school, I couldn't stop talking about how excited I was. My new friend, with an attitude, said, "Trees are dumb. Who cares about them?" As my face turned hot and embarrassingly red, I felt stupid for wanting a tree. What was wrong with me?

The afternoon rolled around, and my teacher began to pass the birch trees out as she discussed our planting instructions again. I had envisioned her giving us a tree taller than I was, wondering how I would carry it on the bus. As my classmates received their trees, I was so disappointed that they were just small sticks the size of my pencil with one or two tiny green leaves poking out of the top. Then my name was called, and I walked up to get mine. *What. The. Heck?* Mine didn't even have the tiny green leaves. It was dead. *This is the dumbest day ever*, I thought.

Earlier that morning, my friend said she was going to throw her tree away, and in this moment, I didn't blame her. In fact, I looked at my dead stick sitting on my desk, and I decided to adopt her plan. The bell rang, and our teacher ensured we all had our trees in hand as we left for the day. The bus driver gave us strict instructions on how to hold the trees until our bus stop. All the adults were watching, so I couldn't throw the stupid stick away. It would have to wait until I got home.

Of course, my mom was waiting for me at the door and couldn't wait to see the birch tree I had happily anticipated. I instantly told her that my tree was dead. "I'm not planting that dead stick," I passionately proclaimed. "Oh yes you are!" she said in her quiet and firm voice. "Now take it down to the rock garden where your dad is waiting for you." My patient dad helped me plant the dead stick and shared his motivational wisdom about growth as I rolled my eyes, and we went on with our evening. Sure enough, within a few days, baby leaves popped out of my stick. I was actually giddy when I saw them. Of course, I never mentioned it to my friend. She would have thought I was a dork for not throwing that stick in the trash.

The following year, my cool-kid friend was placed in a different classroom, I was back to my normal half sass / half respectful attitude, and my tree was growing like crazy. I was so glad that the circumstances and wise adults hadn't allowed me to throw away my tree. Following the popular and cool kids is rarely a good idea, even for grown-ups. It's much better to be uniquely you, even if you are a plant nerd. Especially if you're a plant nerd! Many years later, I still get to visit my towering birch tree when I go to my parents' house.

Family planting and gardening are great ways to build memories, enhance responsibility, and allow the youngsters to express their uniqueness and creativity. It's wonderful to get children involved in deciding what to grow, what varieties, and what colors. You will be giving a priceless gift to the next generation and to all creation. A garden has a way of quickly becoming your favorite happy place to dance to your own beet.

The grace-filled life is an invitation to be yourself and do more of what brings you joy.

PERSONALIZE YOUR CONTAINER SALSA GARDEN

Whether you're in a high-rise condo or on a 100-acre farm, you can have a salsa garden steps from your kitchen. And best of all, you can plant ingredients to sweeten or spice up your salsa recipes. It's all about what you like!

Three simple steps lead you to salsa:

1. Fill a container ¾ full with a soil containing perlite or vermiculite for moisture control. Containers seem to dry out quicker than the ground.

2. Plant what you love! Tomatoes, spicy peppers, green onions, and cilantro are my faves. Prefer sweet? Plant fruit like a mini lime plant, strawberries, or a large indoor mango tree with other salsa plants at the base.

3. Fill it in with additional soil. Place it in the sunshine and water regularly.

When it's time to harvest, call your loved ones to help you pluck and chop your personalized ingredients and enjoy with your favorite tortilla chips or sturdy veggies like carrot chips, celery, or long slices of crisp cucumber.

POTATO TOWER
A.K.A. GARDEN LASAGNA

Planting veggies vertically is a wonderful way to see your produce. Pests will have trouble reaching them, and it's a beautiful space saver. You could even grow produce just outside your apartment door. Just because everyone else grows their potatoes in rows in the ground doesn't mean you can't build a potato tower instead. Use whatever varieties of potatoes your family prefers. We like to change it up every layer, which is why I like to call this a garden lasagna!

SUPPLIES
— 1 square steel fencing, 3–4 feet wide and tall
— Straw
— Garden soil
— 1–2 lbs. seed potatoes per tower

DIRECTIONS
1. Bend some steel fencing into a tube. When you cut the fencing with wire cutters, fold the wire back on itself to catch the other side and fasten to make a cylinder. The top and bottom will be open.
2. Choose a sunny location with good soil drainage for your tower. Securely place one open end on the ground with the other open end facing the sky.
3. Make a nest of straw in the bottom and fill it with a good soil mixture.
4. Nestle 8 seed potatoes, with eyes pointing to the outside, around the circle.
5. Continue building by layering: hay, soil, seed potatoes. Repeat this until you run out of seed potatoes.
6. Put a final topping of soil and hay on top, and you're done. Water generously.

When your potato plants have started to wilt, begin harvesting. Simply push the tower over and pull the potatoes out. It's like mining for gold. Don't forget to reuse your leftover soil in the compost pile or another area of the garden in a rotation.

FROMAGE FOCACCIA GARDEN

Making focaccia can be a piece of art and a stress reliever. You can knead it, punch it, and stab holes in it. Hooray for self-care in the form of scrumptious carbs.

INGREDIENTS FOR BREAD DOUGH

— 3½ cups all-purpose flour
— 2 tsp. instant yeast
— 1½ tsp. salt
— 2 T. olive oil
— 1¼ cups water

INGREDIENTS FOR FILLING

— 1 T. olive oil
— 2 medium-sized beets, thinly sliced
— 3 cups shredded mozzarella
— 1 tsp. salt

INGREDIENTS FOR TOPPINGS

Make it your own custom masterpiece. Here's what we used:
— Chive stalks for flower stems
— Sliced peppers for sunflower petals
— Olives for the sunflower and bees
— Onions for bee wings
— Cherry tomatoes for tall flower stalk
— Parsley, basil, and oregano for leaves and grass
— Radish slices for round flowers

Combine the dough ingredients and then knead. Place the dough in a greased bowl, cover, and allow it to rise for 2 to 3 hours. Transfer it to a floured surface and knead. Divide to form two balls and allow these to rest covered for 15 minutes.

Roll the first ball thin to fit a well-oiled 9 x 13-inch cake pan. Top with a drizzle of olive oil, then beet slices (or try pepperoni), and then shredded mozzarella and salt. Spread the filling, leaving 1 inch around the edges.

Roll the second ball thin to the same shape and then place it on top of the filling layer, pressing the edges together to seal in the filling.

Preheat the oven to 425°. Cover with a slightly damp cloth and allow to rise for 45 minutes. Next, poke gentle indentations into it with your finger without breaking into the filling. Brush the bread with olive oil and begin your gardenscape pushing your toppings into the dough. Sprinkle with salt and bake for 30 to 35 minutes.

Serve warm, the cheese melts into the beets and bread for a delicious artisan bread experience.

CHAPTER SEVEN

A Rescued and Reclaimed Life

Homesteaders are cut from a different cloth than most. We are tough as nails when we need to be, yet we shed a tear when our neighbor loses their cherished hound dog. We love to grow things in the dirt, eat real food, and cultivate lasting relationships, and we get a thrill out of repurposed old treasures. Can I get an amen? Is that you?

We have grit, and there is something special about pursuing the simple life and going back to the basics. Being a good steward of what God has gifted us is important. Taking an object that has been tossed away and restoring it to something beautiful and unexpected can be a rewarding part of this lifestyle.

The Greenhouse Effect

The growing season in the Midwest is limited due to the harsh and frigid winters. We've always dreamed of having a greenhouse to extend our growing season and get a head start on planting. But they are so expensive, so we never took the idea seriously. That is until we came across some amazing old busted-up windows that were begging to be part of a greenhouse. We had a pile of more reclaimed windows and beams in our barn and a set of old French doors that came from a thrift store. Let the building begin.

It is an adventure in creative problem-solving to repurpose building materials. They are old and worn and often beat-up, with gouges and paint chips from varied pasts. And their measurements are never standard sizes! But the secret is to see the potential beauty and worth.

We didn't have any plans for our greenhouse build, so we let the dimensions of our reclaimed materials guide the process. (I told you, homesteaders do their own thing.) We even finished off the floor with leftover paver blocks from our son's farm.

There is an excitement to life when you begin to see things not as they are but as what they could be. Over the years, we've learned the pure joy of what a little vision and a lot of elbow grease can produce. The worn imperfections of an old piece of wood or a window tell a beautiful story of the past and contribute beauty to what is to come.

This Little Light of Mine

The homestead greenhouse is all about light, warmth, and early plant growth. Sunshine is a key ingredient to a thriving greenhouse, as is deep root growth. Inside the space, you will want to cultivate black dirt, nurture tender seedlings, and allow in a full measure of light for germination. Building those deep roots inside the shelter is a game changer. When you move plants outside to the harsh weather, they are established and can survive whatever elements come their way.

A successful greenhouse uses materials that allow the light in. Our greenhouse, built from repurposed materials, allowed us to start our seeds in the warmth and light, even while there was snow still on the ground.

I like to think of myself as one of those broken and chipped windows that God is reclaiming for his building project to let his light and warmth shine through.

A Homestead Rehab

When we moved to our homestead 20 years, ago our finances were tight. When I say tight, I mean not an extra penny for wiggle room. We were a family of six on a fireman's salary, and I was a stay-at-home mom trying to keep my four kiddos fed, happy, and healthy. Our motto was Reduce, Reuse, and Recycle—not because it was trendy or we were environmentalists, but because we were broke. Maybe that made us a dark shade of khaki instead of green, but we repurposed everything we could.

There were literally a thousand projects on our small farm, from the 120-year-old fixer-upper house; to the worn, ugly turkey barn filled with junk; to the little dilapidated shack the previous owners called the carriage house. It sounds much more charming than it was. Our little place had so much potential, but our resources, skills, and knowledge were lacking, to say the least. We were two clueless kids with four babies, and we didn't know anything about anything.

However, we were in love with the idea of living off the land on this property that many told us to bulldoze flat. Our friends and family thought we were crazy for taking on a project this vast without resources, but we didn't listen. Year after year and project after project, we slowly made progress in repurposing and restoring every inch of our homestead. Each night, as we tucked those kiddos in bed and said our prayers, we thanked God for all the blessings he gave us. Even though we were exhausted and our muscles were sore, it felt right. We had found our happy place—and the restoration of this property continues to restore our souls.

In every corner of our property, you'll find treasures built with reclaimed materials that were often free or purchased for minimal cost. The Dutch door in our barn was pulled out of a friend's trash. Our raised garden beds are made from old bookshelves or scrap cedar.

When a tornado ripped through our hometown, heaps of damaged scraps littered the property. It was like a yard sale came to us. Months later, we used the weather-beaten wood to build a treehouse in the back of the property.

Inside our farmhouse, you can see the cedar fireplace mantle made of wood from a friend's farm, the master bath vanity that used to be our dresser, and the range hood made of wood pulled out of a pile in our barn.

I'll admit, over the years there've been moments when I thought CJ had lost his mind when he explained his visions for our small backyard farm. One of those times, he brought a heap of trash lumber home on his trailer and said he was going to expand and rehab the chicken coop. "Have you lost your living mind?" I believe were my exact words.

I was happy with our chicken coop the way it was. It was a tight space for our expanding flock, but it worked. It was an adorable child's playhouse that we converted by adding a nesting box and fenced run. I considered it a huge upgrade from the old deck box we had used for a coop for years. But CJ had found another free kids' playset on Craigslist, and he quickly headed downtown into the city and disassembled it for his future addition to the coop. It turned out fabulous, and I'm a bit embarrassed that I ever doubted his vision.

Our biggest reclaimed project to date was across the lane. Our oldest son purchased the property and barn that sits on five acres. He turned the old barn loft into a beautiful studio workshop full of reclaimed roofing materials on the walls, repurposed storage cabinets, and old windows. Those recycled windows allow him to overlook a beautiful pond. It's a stunning view from the upstairs of the barndominium.

One of my very favorite projects was the restoration of our back field into a small flower farm. That part of our farm was once occupied by an old, janky aboveground pool that was an eyesore. Of course, we did get full pleasure from the swimming fun while the kiddos were smaller, but the metal heap was falling in on itself and probably dangerous. Hooray for reclaiming the dirt for beautiful blooms.

Gathering what comes to us over time and turning what others might call useless, flawed material into the building blocks of our homestead are examples of grace in our everyday lives.

Rescued and Adopted

Most homesteaders would agree that they are in the rescue business, especially when it comes to farm fur babies. Nothing can tug at your heartstrings like a darling animal with sparkling eyes in need of rescuing. We found that out during a community service day with my daughter Sophia's sports team. They volunteered at a pet shelter, and Sophia experienced love at first sight with a tiny white fur ball of a female pup who was in a kennel with nine rowdy brothers. As soon as they placed the sweet pup in Sophia's arms, it looked up with beautiful, trusting eyes and then closed them. Fast asleep, it was apparent she was thankful someone had gotten her out of the chaotic pen. You guessed it. Our day of volunteering became a day of rescuing this little puppy Pyrenees mix, who we named Elsa. We thought we were just rescuing an animal, but in turn, that little white fur ball restored our hearts.

It happens all the time—this connection with creatures that inspires our protective nature. Even to the extent of risky heroics! A while back, CJ and his firemen buddies were building our long-awaited kitchen addition that would finally attach the garage to our family room. One morning, Isaiah, our teenage son, looked out his upstairs bedroom window over the construction and saw a scared, stray cat on the new roof rafter that was 15 feet high.

Of course, without getting approval from his safety-conscious parents, he climbed out of his bedroom window onto the two-story roof, balance beamed across the unstable boards, and rescued the stray. The next day, that little stinker kitty was back up there. And so was my son to rescue her again. Finally, he told us about her and the treacherous rescues. The next two days, I was on the lookout for her, but she was nowhere to be found. It was a holiday weekend, and we were busy prepping for our Easter feast, so I quickly forgot about her.

Then early Easter morning, I was up before the sunrise, anticipating the joy of one of my favorite days of the year. I was looking forward to our Resurrection Sunday church service and a day filled with happy kiddos hyper from their sugar highs, fluffy baby chicks, extended family, delicious food, and the coveted short afternoon nap to sleep off the carb coma (bless it). Does it get any better?

It was rainy and incredibly cold. Until the night before, the forecast had included snow. In the quiet of the early dawn, I pulled freshly washed tablecloths out of the dryer. That's when I heard a faint meow outside. I looked out the window and didn't see a thing, but it was still dark out. I opened the mudroom door, and the chilly rain pelted my face. Oh, the joys of living in construction with part of your home open to the elements. It felt like tiny frozen daggers. Whatever was making those pleas had to be miserable in this blustery weather. I leaned my head out further to listen closely. Knowing I was nearby, the meows intensified and became desperate. And then I spotted the gray construction kitty wedged between the roof rafters about ten feet high. It was stuck halfway in and halfway out of the house, struggling to get free.

I ran back in the house to grab my stepladder, climbed right up, and finagled the soaked and pathetic kitty out of the drenched boards. Once free, she gave me the sweetest and softest meow, as if to say, "Thank you, I've been waiting for you." I clumsily reentered the house, banging into the doorjamb with a step ladder in one arm and a soaked and skinny kitty clinging for life in my other.

Once inside, I grabbed a fluffy towel and wrapped it around the drowned rat—I mean, kitty. Just then, Sophia burst into the room, her face aglow as soon as she saw this gift from God literally dropped from above. There was no hiding the kitty or faking a stern list of reasons we couldn't have yet another animal. Now that Sophia was in the know, there was a new member of the family.

The grace-filled life reclaims worn imperfections and restores them into a masterpiece.

The kitten was stiff, but as we dried it off and snuggled close, a loud purr let us know all was well. Within the hour, it was playing and then napping in Sophie's arms. Since that day many years ago, they've been inseparable. She's already making plans to sneak Easter into her college dorm. Of course, I won't let that happen because I'm a good rule follower! (And because that silly kitty stole my heart, and I don't want Easter to move out.)

Sometimes we view ourselves or others as heaps of discarded, rough, and splintered lumber, but God sees his children as stunning perfection. If you've been around me much, you know I'm not a fan of striving for perfection. However, when we accept God's grace over our mess, he views us as priceless treasures. He can take our scattered pieces and rubble and create something beautiful, purposeful, and joy-filled with the most unlikely of materials of our past and our flaws.

The worn imperfections of your life can tell the story of redemption. God is in the restoration business. He can see past the multitude of mistakes and use the gouges in the wood to make us his masterpiece. No matter what you've done or who you've hurt, you can be restored to an exquisite work of art. The faith journey with God has it all, my friend. We are reclaimed, restored, and adopted by the One who loves unconditionally and makes all things new in his grace.

GREENHOUSE WITH RECLAIMED MATERIALS

A greenhouse is a magical place and will allow you to start your plants early. When using reclaimed materials such as old windows and doors, you can keep your pocketbook happy and plants thriving.

SUPPLIES
— Reclaimed wood, windows, doors, etc.
— Cement
— 4 posts
— Clear plastic sheeting

DIRECTIONS

1. Determine a location. You will want the greenhouse to have full sun and be near a water source.

2. Determine the size of the structure based on your property and materials.

3. Lay out all the reclaimed windows, lumber, and doors to see if you have enough. If not, ask around. Shop antique or thrift stores for more. Four tall and solid corner posts are important.

4. Dig your corner post holes, add the posts, and mix 1 bag of cement for each hole. Secure the posts so they are level and straight. Wait for the cement to dry completely before the next steps.

5. Add your reclaimed windows and doors in whatever positions you like. Secure them with screws to the solid corner posts first and then to each other.

6. Create your roof with sturdy, clear plastic sheeting. Secure it to the corner posts and top windows with screws. We don't recommend glass on the roof, especially if you get hail in your planting zone.

7. Leave the floor dirt or add reclaimed bricks and pavers.

8. Add a potting bench and plants.

Don't worry about gaps between your old building materials. Ventilation and airflow are important in a greenhouse.

STRAWBERRY POUND CAKE TOWER

Every summer, my mama would serve us fresh strawberries on top of a buttery pound cake. My version of this recipe was adapted from the historical butter pound cake named after the measurement needed for each of the four ingredients, a pound each. I also add sour cream and vanilla for moistness. It makes a large amount of batter, and the delicious treat was often shared with multiple homesteading families. Feel free to cut the recipe in half if you're only serving your family.

INGREDIENTS FOR POUND CAKE

— 1 lb. (4 sticks) butter
— 1 lb. (2 cups) sugar
— 1 lb. (9 large) eggs
— 1 lb. (4 cups) flour
— 2 T. vanilla
— $\frac{3}{4}$ cup sour cream

INGREDIENTS FOR TOPPING

— 3 pints (6 cups) strawberries
— 1 cup sugar
— 16 oz. whipped cream

DIRECTIONS FOR POUND CAKE

Preheat the oven to 350°. Butter and flour two 8-inch round pans.

Beat the softened butter in a stand mixer on medium until creamy and then add sugar and sour cream. Mix for 2 minutes.

Add the eggs to the butter mixture. Add the vanilla and then the flour gradually, ½ a cup at a time. Beat for an additional 2 minutes.

Spread the batter evenly in the prepared pans. Bake for 45 minutes. Let them cool for 20 minutes, then invert the pound cakes onto a cooling rack. Let them cool for an hour in the refrigerator before cutting.

Use a long, serrated knife to cut off the top of the cakes to make them flat. Then create two layers from each cake by slicing them in half horizontally

DIRECTIONS FOR STRAWBERRY TOPPING

Wash the strawberries, remove the stems, and cut the berries in half. Mix with sugar and refrigerate for at least 1 hour while juices develop.

Assemble the tower in layers, starting with the cake, then the strawberry mixture, and finally the whipped cream. Repeat this process three more times. Top with a couple of whole strawberries with stems as a garnish.

CHAPTER EIGHT

Setting Intentions and the Dinner Table

Years ago when we decided to pursue the authentic, simple life, we realized the importance of being intentional with our time and resources. Slow living on a homestead is hard work that needs to be planned out a year in advance. When planting the vineyard and orchard, we understood that a full harvest was a couple of years away. A summer vegetable bounty is mapped out the year prior by prepping the soil and starting seeds indoors over the winter.

And in this life of instant gratification, same-day deliveries, and distracting technology in our hands, the same focus and planning are required to raise up the next generation and build a strong family with the values we deem important. I say to set intentions like you set a table—*before* life starts serving up its offerings for the day. Whether we're sharing a meal or details about our day, doing chores or homework, being intentional gives meaning to the simple times.

Gather Round the Table

I truly believe a family's dining table is one of the most important places to create intention. Our homestead table is huge, bulky, and in need of another good sanding, but it fits our lifestyle and is priceless to us. It will forever inspire our family to gather because it is the heart of the home where we're nourished not only with food but with laughter, tears, traditions, and grace.

It is also where we teach by example the importance of intention and connection. At our table, the kids know to remove their hats. We pray, break bread, make plans, and harass someone about their need for a haircut, and there are always fire station stories, which are a bit like exaggerated fishing stories because each one seems bigger and more dramatic than the next.

To preserve this sacred time with family, years ago we started the tradition of Sunday supper. It may look different week to week for our family. One week we may be headed to Grandma's house for ham and beans, and then the following it is back to ours for barbecue or the traditional "Sunday Pot." We can't always be together, but we preserve it as a goal. This circles back to choosing to be intentional and making a plan that supports what we value. This is how traditions are created and how something as simple as a shared meal around an old table forms a foundation that holds a family close.

When adversity strikes, having a base of daily faith, healthy habits, chores, and meal rituals can be the glue that holds life together. If you are on the struggle bus and the last wheel is falling off the axel, you can face all your fears and troubles with a strong family unit.

If you aren't scheduling regular meals with your friends and family, it's never too late to start. Keep it simple. Occasionally we set the table like fancy folks, but most of the time it's pretty basic. Our centerpiece is usually a pot of soup and wildflowers from the field outside or even vintage fire gear when Sunday supper turns into celebrating a fire academy graduation. Centering family time around our table has been purposeful. Making it a habit is a big reason we have such close-knit relationships. Families can be messy and irritating, yet the raw, unedited conversations that happen over supper bring souls together and build a heritage that can't be taken away.

Table Talk

We consider ourselves extra blessed because a legacy of shared tales and memories is engrained in the rough, imperfect wood of our treasured farm table. It was saved from an old fire station that had been closed for years and was entrusted to us by another firefighter family. With CJ as the fire chief and all three boys following in his footsteps as firefighters, it makes this table extra special. I have no doubt that it will be a part of our family for generations.

Oh, if this table could talk and share the stories it has heard! It's humbling to think of the healing conversations that have happened after tragic community emergency calls, the fire that claimed a brilliant chief, and the on-duty deaths of revered firefighters. The prayers and tales were exchanged late into the night, with hearts broken and mended at the table. And I guarantee you that much mischief was also planned and carried out around the table over the years—from bottle rocket fights in the station kitchen to laughing about pulling donut pranks on neighboring city crews.

It is at the table that we enjoy birthday dinners for each family member. We feed babies their first mashed-up bananas, grab a quick burger before a youth sports meet, continue to complain about a high school wrestling coach, and banter about which university is best and if college is even needed these days.

More recently, the dinner table activities have been wedding planning, grieving Gramps's passing, learning of a new grandbaby, and then now feeding that precious little one mashed-up bananas. This is the good stuff, y'all—life's simple joys and sorrows being shared with your people. Encouraging these conversations and interactions makes life rich. If you have this connection in your home, you are as wealthy as a millionaire, regardless of what your bank statement says.

The circle of life within generations happens every day, right in front of our eyes at the blessed kitchen table. Don't blink or you'll miss it.

Today's Menu Is Take It or Leave It

Early pioneers and the firefighters who sat around our table all those years have a lot of similarities. The original homesteaders did not stray far from their initial plans and rules because their lives depended on them. Their supplies, trails, and responsibilities were mapped out with precision. Everyone had an important job to do, and the survival of the community was the priority.

Firefighters on the job work very similarly. There are daily chores and a few unwritten rules that everyone is aware of. They are a bit comical, and there are even a couple worth adopting.

When firefighters work a 24-hour shift, each fire station has a designated cook (the boss of the day), and then there is a bull cook (the servant of the day). The cook plans the menu and ensures the proper ingredients are purchased by the other members of the cook shack. The bull cook is stuck with all the chopping and prep work. They start prepping the meal early so if the crew catches a call, like they always do, they can just turn off the burners as they are running to the rig. Foodies and world-class chefs can't hold a candle to their delicious recipes.

Here's something you might want to enforce at your dinner table: One of the unwritten station rules is "Never complain about what is on the menu." If a crew member makes a snarky remark about dinner, they are kicked out of the cook shack for a year. Of course, there is even a ritual for getting kicked out. The cook will smash the complainer's plate on the hard floor, breaking it into pieces, signaling they're out and will be brown bagging it for a while.

Whenever one of our family members makes a comment about what I'm cooking, I giggle to myself and envision throwing their plate on the ground. I haven't done this yet, but I feel my time is coming.

If You Can't Take the Heat, Get Out of the Kitchen

If you're stressed and overworked (and more than a little tempted to throw plates daily), your family will feel the tension. It may be time to retreat from your chores and responsibilities for a bit and come up with a new plan. Listen to your body and learn to recognize when you need a break. Intentional living grounds our souls during instability and brings purpose and joy to the family. Once you have yourself organized and in place, it's easier to help bring order to the rest of your family. You need to make sure you are healthy mentally and physically in order to be the best you can be for your family.

In the coop, I've watched the hens' interactions with their newborn chicks. The mamas spend endless hours fluffing their bedding, making sure the chicks are fed and warm. When all are sleeping, the mama hen sneaks off to refuel her own fluids, scratch grains, and grab some fresh air. Within minutes, the littles are out following her around again, but she is refreshed and ready to take on the world. Making time for yourself will help everyone around you. A flower in the garden can't always be blooming—it needs to rest and replenish its nutrients during the seasonal cycles to prepare for the beauty to come. We need to rest and replenish just as our plants do.

My lifeline is my daily planner. Ordering my decisions and actions helps me live in peace. Sleeping, Bible reading, exercising, food planning, taking supplements, and drinking plenty of water always top off my daily to-do list. Then I add the other items that need my attention and time. When the list gets too long, it's time to shed some responsibilities, take a breather, and unplug from technology. Doing so replenishes my soul and allows me to focus on what's important. If you want to make the people in your life feel important, put down your phone.

Life can be so exciting and demanding, making it easy to overschedule yourself or your kids. If you have a talented youngster in your home, it's hard not to throw all your time and money at their lessons, practices, and events, which keeps adding to the exhaustion and overwhelm.

Our kiddos were all three-sport athletes and pursued many other outside activities, and my rear end was numb sitting in the bleachers year around, cheering on my littles. These activities teach social skills, the benefits of healthy exercise, and how to win and lose gracefully, but they shouldn't be the entire focus for your kids. The same is true for any extracurricular activities. A heritage and identity that is centered on their faith, family, and home will keep them grounded if they blow out a knee at practice or get cut from the orchestra. That's a gift of the intentional life. It isn't about plans unfolding perfectly; it's about shaping an authentic life that supports you even when they don't.

The Importance of a Morning Routine

Most homesteaders understand the importance of the morning routine because if it isn't carried out, their flock and herd will quickly and loudly let them know it's not acceptable. Toby, our turkey who thinks he is a rooster, will jump up on top of the coop to wake the world up with his gaggling until all the outdoor chores are complete. Our farm dogs and kitty are not much different in their methods of letting us know when we are running late for their breakfast time.

I'm an early riser. I treasure a few quiet minutes to myself as the sun peeks over the horizon, before the family and animals are awake and active. To line up with our desire to have a simple and intentional life, we created a plan to pass on the joy of a peaceful morning to our kiddos. Whether kids are getting on a school bus, in virtual classes, or homeschooled, mornings can be chaotic. Honestly, it can be the worst hour of the day if you're not intentional about it.

We realized after our first two kids became teens there was a shift happening in the world set off by more access to technology, the prevalence of social media, and the increase in youth mental health issues such as substance abuse, bullying,

cutting, and eating disorders. Sometimes it seemed as if every day brought news of another sweet kid from a solid family we knew who was dealing with tragic concerns. These kiddos and their friends were being bombarded with serious adult problems, and here I was nagging my kids about what they wore to school and bringing their dirty socks down to the laundry bin.

It was time for us to make an intentional shift in parenting. We wanted to raise up the next generation of our family happy, healthy, and confident in Christ. Through the trial and error of raising four kids, we stumbled upon a simple recipe for peaceful mornings to ease the morning routine and strengthen each child's sense of God's presence in their life. This intentional approach makes it easier for a child to get ready and join the breakfast table, even if briefly, and it helps you eliminate the morning chaos so you send your child to face the world full of joy, truth, and godly wisdom.

A Recipe for Peaceful Mornings with Kids

Parenting our sassy and strong-willed kiddos is the most important and hardest thing we can do on this planet. As the happy little ones transition to school-aged kids, a morning routine becomes even more important. When we turn the focus away from the activity accolades, external appearances, and what the Jones's kids are doing, it is life-giving for the next generation. This simple morning routine, which begins the night before, will bring peace to you and your kids.

1. **Set consistent times.** Have a regular window of time planned for play and homework so your child's evening makes the next morning easier. An hour before bed, check in to make sure all their homework is finished.

2. **Do next-day task reminders before bedtime.** Keep the questions simple. For example, "Do you have your uniform in your backpack for the sports

meet after school?" Before they go to sleep, have all tomorrow's important items ready.

3. **Remove phones from the bedroom.** Yes, you read that right. Spend $15 on a real alarm clock for your children and have them wake up without a phone. Kids (and adults, for that matter) are not mature enough to set their phone boundaries, and the all-night chats and phone notifications impact their health. Steady sleep is critical while their brains are developing. This is the hardest step but is the most rewarding when put in place. Mama, you can do this.

4. **Enter parent morning-warrior mode.** Wake up 30 minutes early to put on strong coffee, light a candle, and play low-level, soothing music. Christian worship and folkie spa playlists are the favorites around here. Get your act together so you can be fully present during the important breakfast time. Put your phone and other distractions away. This way, you can set the tone for your family and a peaceful day.

5. **Let preteens and teens choose their clothes.** Focus on what is going on internally with them and try not to care so much about what they wear, unless it is inappropriate. Let it go. It's not a battle worth fighting. The school halls are filled with teens in shorts when snow is on the ground. Chances are they will wise up on their own eventually.

6. **Set a consistent breakfast time.** At our house, food is a big motivator, so when I told the kids they couldn't eat breakfast until they were completely ready, they complained, rolled their eyes, and then, of course, got ready quickly. I'm not above bribery!

7. **Read a devotion.** Once our wild kids sat down to eat, I took the opportunity to read to them, instilling peace and wisdom with a two-minute Bible devotion while they were shoveling down their eggs. It didn't seem like it was making a difference, but it was soaking in and making way for questions and conversations later in the day…and later in life.

8. **Gather for hug and prayer time.** When the kids were dressed and fed, school bags ready, I would say, "Give me a hug." Then I prayed a quick prayer out loud over them while we hugged. Here is an example: "Lord Jesus, keep them safe and healthy today. Let them be kind, feel your presence, and hear your voice in their ears." Then I'd add something about what they're dealing with, such as an upcoming math test.

   Humor never hurts. Start singing "Jesus, Take the Wheel" after a minor fender bender the week prior. Your kids will act like they don't want this hug prayer. Do it anyway. When you intentionally make this part of the routine, they'll start coming to you when they need to leave. Bless your babies and tell them you love them. *Every. Single. Day.* Even when they are taller than you.

Whether you gather your loved ones around a table or around a plan, the balance of grace and discipline will encourage them daily. It's our job as parents to ignite the desire for a relationship with God, not hit them over the head with a list of can and can't do activities. When you focus on the matters of the heart, your family is less likely to complain about what life serves up. The hardships, detours, and interruptions are transformed by and into the good life, the grace-filled life.

Prayer. Love. Intention. God's direction. Repeat.

FAMILY COMMAND CENTER

Scheduling activities, planning mealtimes, preparing scratch recipes together, and limiting morning chaos can ground our souls during instability and bring purpose and joy to the family. A family command center can help you prioritize and organize the chaos.

SUPPLIES
— Wall location near the home entrance or kitchen
— Master family calendar
— Containers and hooks for each kiddo (file holders, cubbies or bag hooks)
— Power strip for charging

DIRECTIONS
1. Pick a location near the kitchen or home entrance.
2. Hang a master calendar for activities and meal menus.
3. Add family-specific resources such as a chore organizer, goal list, or prayer board.
4. Place file holders for each family member's important papers that need attention.
5. Add backpack hooks, power strips for electronic charging, or cubbies as needed.

Our set of vintage lockers works great for a command center. Get creative with what you have available.

MEATBALLS AND RED SAUCE (A.K.A. THE SUNDAY STATION POT)

With four firefighters in our immediate family, the traditional Sunday fire station pot is a staple that is shared at our place and every firehouse across the city. It feeds a full fire station of 14 adults. Invite your neighbors over, or cut the recipe in half.

INGREDIENTS FOR SAUCE

3 lbs. ground mild Italian
   pork sausage
3 T. olive oil
3 T. garlic, minced
2 onions, diced
4 (12 oz.) cans tomato paste
1 (29 oz.) can crushed tomatoes
3 (29 oz.) cans tomato sauce
2 cups basil
6 (29 oz.) cans water
1 T. black pepper
2 T. salt
$\frac{1}{4}$ tsp. cayenne pepper
$1\frac{1}{2}$ cups sugar

INGREDIENTS FOR MEATBALLS

2 T. garlic, minced
1 onion, diced
$\frac{1}{2}$ bundle parsley, diced
6 lbs. ground beef
3 lbs. ground pork
6 cups bread crumbs
16 oz. grated parmesan or
   Romano cheese
3 tsp. salt
3 tsp. pepper
12 eggs
2 cups water
Vegetable oil

DIRECTIONS FOR SAUCE

Brown the sausage in a skillet.

   Heat up a large saucepan and coat it with the olive oil. Add the garlic and diced onion and sauté until translucent. Add the tomato paste to the onion and garlic and simmer for 5 minutes. Add the crushed tomatoes, tomato sauce, basil, water, pepper, salt, cayenne, sugar, and sausage. Cook on high for 15 minutes, then reduce the heat and simmer for 4 to 6 hours.

DIRECTIONS FOR MEATBALLS

Combine all the ingredients into large mixing bowl. Use an ice cream scoop to form the meatballs. Heat ½ inch of oil to 350° and fry until brown.

Bake at 400° for 25 minutes. Turn the meatballs continuously until done.

Serve with your favorite pasta, salad, and garlic bread.

CHAPTER NINE

Fireflies and the Front Porch

Imperfectly perfect outdoor gatherings are a wonderful way to connect and build memories with your loved ones. There is something special about breaking bread outside with your favorite people. Such an experience is usually more casual than an indoor gathering and creates breathing room for the authentic conversations and relationships we're hungry for.

Honest entertaining with simple menus, table settings, string lighting, and ease of cleanup are important when gathering with family and friends at the homestead. Combining nature and hospitality with food, friends, and family is a priceless gift because it helps you shed your perfectionism and enjoy those you love.

Brave Beginnings

In the early years of our marriage, I realized just how different two people in love can be. I was the overanalyzing play-it-safe girl, and CJ was the wild risk-taker. On every vacation, he was dragging me to the next extreme adventure—one I likely didn't want to participate in because I'd read an article about someone losing an arm doing that very thing.

We've climbed to the tops of mountains and dived to the depths of the sea, once even with whale sharks the size of school buses. Yet strangely enough, planning a simple dinner party at my own home was more terrifying than swimming with the sharks! For a recovering perfectionist that spends time online looking for ideas on comparison apps filled with stunning pictures and foodie recipes, the expectations I made for myself were too high. In addition, if you are like me and on a tight budget (no cleaning service, party planner, or caterer here!), it can be overwhelming to manage it all.

For many, the anxiety of hosting an outdoor gathering begins at the thought of unruly weather, since it falls under the "can't control" list. Perfectionists and even semi-perfectionists hate the loss of *that* control. There are bugs, rain clouds, and temperature fluctuations that may throw you for a loop. If you can lower your expectations and shift your thoughts to the people coming, there is much more fun to be had. An event in nature should be about your relationships with others, true hospitality, and soaking up God's creation, not about a Pinterest-worthy photo.

Embrace Imperfections

I have found in my life that true happiness can't coexist with striving for perfection. That perfectionist lifestyle is based on pride and the fear of not being good enough. Let that crap go and embrace the imperfections. I often cling to the concept of God's grace…loving us despite our pasts, flaws, and mess-ups. That is why we named our small farm the Grace-Filled Homestead. It's not a place where we have it all together but a picture of God's grace, a manure-filled mess, and lots of joy.

Let's practice self-grace, feel God's grace, and embrace the intention for your next gathering, not the perfection of it. These ideas can help you ease into your next hosted event.

Location and Table

Experiment with the best location for your gathering. It can be in your backyard, on the front porch, or behind your barn. Use a sturdy table for the foundation of your event. We have pulled out an old kitchen table with benches. Others have made a table out of sawhorses and a sheet of plywood. A pallet with pillows on the ground for seating adds an extra cozy vibe to your brunch. We chose the chicken coop as a backdrop for our fall dinner. This allowed us to use the electrical outlets for lighting and music.

Lighting

Adding string overhead lights to your dinner space improves the atmosphere immediately, especially for an evening dinner party. You can secure your light strand to a corner of a barn or even wrap it around a tree branch. Plug in extension cords for the electricity. If you want to go full rustic, you can place votives all around your table for a candlelit night under the stars. Of course, the fireflies are always welcome guests.

Guest List and Engagement

Decide how many you are inviting and reach out to them. Is this strictly friends or family as well? Think about seating and who you will want to seat next to each other. It can be fun to play cupid with your guests at a cozy evening dinner party. Fill your friends and family in on the plans and ask them to bring a local farm-to-table dish, garden party dessert, or appetizer.

Table Setting and Music

Keep the decor and place settings simple so you can focus on your guests and enjoy the gathering yourself. For a harvest dinner, a few pumpkins or gourds on the table are all you need. A fresh floral centerpiece could be the focal point of a morning garden brunch. The food and drinks are the main decor. Determine your music play-list and delivery system, and remember that music sets the tone and atmosphere for your gathering. A friend with a folkie voice and guitar is worth their weight in gold.

Menu

It's time to decide if this gathering is appetizers in the garden, a breakfast brunch at the picnic table, or a five-course meal. Of course, my favorite is a bonfire with brats and s'mores. If you are planning a full dinner, there is a new trend emerging. Farm-to-fork dinners are sought-after events for foodies. Many of these hosts ask each guest to bring a farm-to-table dish. If the guests don't have a garden to pick from, they are encouraged to hit the local farmers market or vegetable stand for their ingredients. The joint effort is part of the fun, and you will be surprised by the wonderful dishes your guests bring.

Here's our favorite farm-to-table menu:

Apple cider tea
Baby spinach salad with bacon-wrapped goat cheese
Rosemary potatoes
Seared beef tenderloin skewers
Honey corn bread with blackberry honey butter
Orchard apple pie

Drinks

It's a good idea to serve a seasonal signature drink and offer chilled water. You can get creative with the drink dispensers, pitchers, and glasses. This is a wonder-ful way to enhance the decor element as well. Fruit-infused tea is a great garden brunch drink. Depending on the temperature, you could also offer an after-dinner coffee or hot chocolate.

Food Prep and Service

Most likely, you are preparing part of the food somewhere else and bringing it out to your gathering. Keep that in mind when you are planning. Do you have a large covered pan that can hold the main dish and vegetables? Do your dishes have lids to keep them warm? If your outdoor function is in the heat of summer, you may want to serve cold pasta dishes and chilled fruit. The more you simplify the food, the more fun you will have as the host.

Guest Instructions

As your guests arrive, guide them. Decide if you want to serve them a drink or if they can help themselves. Also, give them a job and get them involved. Tell your guests where you want their dish to go, if they brought one. Direct them to the cheese tray or other appetizer. Ah, glorious cheese. Could there be a better start to a gathering? I think not.

Cleanup

Your outdoor gatherings are for enjoying, even if you are the host. Keep it simple so the cleanup is minimal. If your guests are bringing a dish, they will be leaving with it as well. Bless it. That will cut down on your cleanup time. Have a large bin or wagon nearby to place your dirty dishes and linens in at the end of the night. Make sure it gets back to the house, and it can wait on your attention until morning.

Weather Contingency Plans

Outdoor gatherings do come with a weather risk, and that's usually precipitation. You may want to plan an alternate location, such as the barn or garage. Spend time connecting with your guests to let them know the situation. Keeping a smile on your face and humor in your words will make a lasting impact on those that are joining you. Lighten up and have fun regardless of the weather.

If you are in a condo or apartment building or are limited on patio space, check your local options for an outdoor gathering spot. Many apartment buildings have rooftops or shared green spaces you can reserve. Is there an urban public garden in your area where you can meet for a tour, cocktails, and appetizers? Wherever your gathering is held, pull fresh ingredients from your patio container or garden and treat your favorite people to delicious foodie bites.

Eating fresh and local food prepared in your community adds an extra element of enjoyment to an outdoor gathering. A spring breakfast brunch in your garden will allow your friends and family to enjoy the scents of your flower blooms. An evening dinner among the sparkle string lights and fireflies can be magical. Your guests can be involved by bringing a dish, and you, the host, can enjoy every minute of the evening. A cozy gathering with your favorite people is a wonderful way to fully experience the seasons. It should become a new tradition.

Gatherings to Remember

Many families like to build outdoor gatherings into their annual holiday traditions or milestones. Our gatherings have included a scavenger hunt on Easter, a football game in the yard after the Thanksgiving meal, and roasting chestnuts over the fire while listening to Nat King Cole's holiday classics around Christmas. Even in the colder temperatures, we enjoy the outdoor gatherings by bundling up.

Our personal favorite gatherings at the Grace-Filled Homestead have been the barbecue graduation parties of our children. In late spring, the weather is beautiful, and we all can't wait to get outside and enjoy the smoked meat and desserts while we celebrate the accomplishments of high school. The grandparents, extended family, a few teachers, and lots of high schoolers have joined in the fun. The evening always ends with the kids playing volleyball and making s'mores around the bonfire.

A graduation celebration is a time to display the letter jackets, awards, and the sweetest baby pictures to embarrass the kids a bit. Let's not forget this is also a

celebration of the parents' accomplishments. Our child passed with a diploma and never got suspended or carried off to jail. There was one close call on a suspension, but we squeaked through only because the principal loved our son and said the other kid had it coming. In-school suspension doesn't count as a real suspension, right? Anyway, we made it through all four kids.

Our daughter, Sophia, was the fourth and final kiddo to graduate. Let's be honest—by the time the last kid becomes a senior, parents are over it. Your rear end is numb from sitting in the bleachers, you're tired of dragging yourself to teacher conferences, and the thought of another awards banquet makes you cry. It was February, and we were on the road to watch Sophia compete at a sporting competition hours away. She had left with the high school team earlier that morning.

During the car ride, CJ and I discussed all the spring events leading up to her graduation and even joked about how nice it would be to get our weekends back from the school-dominated calendar. Then he made a profound statement: "The Stenners always finish strong. Let's make this special for her." It was like a marathon runner hitting the wall at mile 22 and committing to make the distance.

Little did we know that in a month, the school would be shut down, and she would never walk the halls again due to the pandemic. The 2020 graduates are a special generation that were born as our nation recovered from the 9/11 tragedy and then graduated during a worldwide pandemic. Their proms, graduation ceremonies, and celebration parties were all canceled.

As the only daughter after three rowdy boys, Sophia was tough. And any kid growing up on a homestead learns grit and perseverance from a young age. She handled the disappointment of losing her senior year much better than her parents did. Our baby girl needed closure and deserved a celebration. As the social distancing regulations were lifted, it was time to party. Hers would be a graduation party to remember.

When Life Gives You Lemons, Make Pink Lemonade!

We were determined to make the evening a celebration that was made just for her and her friends. Sophia has always loved lemonade, so a tart strawberry lemonade was the first thing on the graduation party menu, and the theme was a flower market. CJ had built me a flower cart for Mother's Day, so we pulled it up to the porch area and filled it with blooms for her besties. Of course, smoked meat was on the menu, the s'mores firepit was rolling, and volleyball would round out the evening with those precious kids. This generation is witty, bold, and full of perseverance. I have no doubt they will prevail. Sophia's senior year was less than perfect, but there were joys to be found in the imperfections. Talk about the ultimate senior skip day.

The sound of teenagers giggling while roasting marshmallows for their s'mores, storytelling around the fire pit, and playing a competitive volleyball match in the yard was a melody that we all cherished that evening. Sophia's outdoor graduation party was a magical night to celebrate the end of her senior year.

B Stands for Better Living

Are you still skeptical? Does the thought of hosting an upcoming holiday or milestone celebration make your heart rate soar? Please believe me, friends and family don't care about a perfectly curated gathering. They want real connection and hospitality. Letting go of your idealism is liberating.

A few years ago, I was asked to teach a business class at the local university. I feel so strongly about ditching perfection that I may shock you with my next statement: A+ perfection is overrated, and the best life happens at a B- level.

Yes, even a college professor agrees that a joyfully earned B- is better than a book-smart A+. If the A you're going for ends up representing anxiety and approval, it isn't going to result in anything worth having. I would much rather my students learn real-world applications, take risks in their papers and assignments, and enjoy the process than toil over getting a perfect score. Sometimes you just have to go for it and learn along the way. Don't be afraid to make mistakes. That is where true learning, enjoyment, and magic happen. That is where real and better living happen.

This concept holds true for homesteaders and homesteaders at heart. Several of our friends have been talking about raising chickens for years. They have

The grace-filled life is brave and embraces
the beauty of imperfections.

researched every breed, coop, and watering system. They have purchased chicken courses, bought books, and subscribed to too many YouTube channels about raising chickens, but they have yet to do it.

There is a time to stop building book knowledge and jump in. Maybe that's you right now, so I hope this message is the encouragement you need today to nudge you forward. Homesteaders have a gritty can-do attitude and a willingness to figure things out as we go. We are okay starting with a B- the first season, and then by next season, we're ready to go to the top of the class...or the coop!

When I see that pearly-gate finish line this side of heaven, I will not be in a scar-free, beautifully preserved body—I will be sliding in sideways, muddy, smiling, and flush-faced, having made lots of embarrassing mistakes following my dreams. And I'll be cheering on the others nearby shouting, "Just go for it...stop waiting for things to be perfect!"

This is a good mindset to have in all aspects of life. Go for it and stop waiting until everything is lined up perfectly. Apply to that college, reach out to that interesting person, start that business, apologize without knowing how that person will respond, buy that small farm when you don't know a thing about gardening, or set the date for a big neighborhood block party or family reunion picnic. Then ask yourself, What is the worst thing that could happen?

An outdoor gathering is simple. Friend, let's lighten up, pour some sweet tea, and make some outdoor memories.

A SIMPLE S'MORES STATION

Roasting s'mores around a firepit is a wonderful way to conclude any outdoor party. The casual crunch of the graham crackers followed by the sticky sweet center of melted goodness is pure joy. Let's make a s'mores station for your next gathering:

- Load up a large glass apothecary jar with fluffy marshmallows.
- Place the chocolate bars and graham crackers in two other jars with lids.
- Get creative. Add filling options such as peanut butter cups, cherry mash, and mint chocolates.
- Fill a menu board with fun combination suggestions.
- Display your roasting skewers and wet wipes for the predictable sticky mess.
- Light up your fire pit or Sterno gel cans in a tray of decorative rocks.
- Remember to embrace the imperfections and sticky gooey mess. Enjoy!

STRING-LIGHT FLOWER PLANTER

String lights add an instant cozy glow to an evening gathering. Combine with a planter, and you have a vibrant, sparkling structure that will add ambience and light to any outdoor get-together.

SUPPLIES
— 10-gal. flower planter
— Concrete mix
— 8-foot 4 x 4-inch post
— Hook and lights
— Potting soil and plants

DIRECTIONS

1. Add a bag of dry concrete mix to fill half the planter.

2. Add water from your garden hose until you have an oatmeal consistency. Mix with a shovel.

3. Place the post in the center of the wet concrete. Screw scrap lumber to the post to stabilize it upright until it sets, usually within 24 hours.

4. Drill a couple of drainage holes in the planter.

5. Add planting soil and plants to the top of the planter. Water the plants thoroughly.

6. Install a hook at the top of your post and string your light strand.

Plug in your lights and delight in the coziest spot around!

SEARED BEEF TENDERLOIN ON ROSEMARY SKEWERS

This simple beef skewer recipe has only 8 ingredients. It's delicious served as an appetizer for a large group or a main course in a dinner for 6.

INGREDIENTS

— 3 lbs. filet steaks, 1 to 2 inches thick
— 24 4-inch rosemary stems
— $\frac{1}{4}$ cup olive oil
— 2 T. Worcestershire sauce
— 1 T. brown sugar, packed
— 1 tsp. garlic powder
— 2 tsp. mustard powder
— 3 T. cooking oil to coat the pan

DIRECTIONS

Cube meat into 2-inch pieces and skewer 3 or 4 cubes on each rosemary sprig. In a separate bowl, create the marinade with the olive oil, Worcestershire sauce, brown sugar, garlic powder, and mustard powder. Place the meat skewers in a shallow dish. Pour the marinade over them, coating every piece. Let them sit for 1 hour.

Add cooking oil to a hot skillet, coating the bottom of the pan. Sear the meat skewers for 1 minute on each side or until done. Serve with a sauce of your choice.

CHAPTER TEN

Tire Swinging on the Family Tree

Here at the Grace-Filled Homestead, we cherish our heritage and traditions. Lolah Woods, my Nonnie, was a force of nature and beaming with light. She led a life of mission and service to others, always planting seeds of goodness. She was born in 1900, grew up on a homestead in Missouri, and lost half her high school graduating class to the Spanish flu in 1918. Times were tough, but she was tougher.

After she and my grandpa married, they made their way to settle in Gallup, New Mexico. It was the Wild West, filled with cowboys, Indian reservations, and gritty living. Our family was known for wild rodeos on Saturday night and singing hymns at church on Sunday morning. Although Lolah Woods was tough, she had a soft spot in her heart for the hurting and hungry in her small Western town on Route 66.

Mission Fields at Home

Nonnie would give you the shirt off her back if you needed it, and she often literally did. It may have been the sweater or coat she was wearing, but if you were cold and in need, it was yours and there was no need to return it. There was a large transient community where she lived. She spent most of her mornings at the mission shelter feeding and helping those in need, but it was in the afternoon that I witnessed her true work begin. Her kitchen was the hub of the house. She had a bright red diner booth for her kitchen table set, and the walls and dishes were covered in strawberries.

It would start just after lunch. A thundering bang, bang on the front door. She would escort a woman, man, or full family in to sit at the kitchen table. Every day was different. Nonnie would take her time making them a sandwich while she sang hymns or asked about their day.

She would weigh in on how they could improve their lives, and then she would bring their food to the table. As they started to dig in, she would remind them about the prayer before she would give a simple blessing to God over the food and their lives. Then while they ate, she would ask them if she could read some scriptures of love to them. They snarfed down those sandwiches and headed for the door in only a few minutes. She blessed them personally through her conversation, advice, singing, and Scripture.

She impacted hundreds of people over the years, planting her seeds of love and faith. I remember overhearing my parents chatting about how they were worried someone would hurt her when family wasn't around. She would brush them off and said she was the one to reach them with God's love. My Nonnie was pure brilliant light to everyone that was blessed enough to come into contact with her.

Lolah was a legend, spitfire, and wonderful mentor and passed her giving and loving spirit down to her kids, grandkids, and community. There was no room for the typical religious church-lady judgment in her mission. She loved people just as they were. Letting Christ's light shine through by remaining sensitive to the needs of others can be a source of warmth and comfort for those who need it the most. The

lost and hurting will rarely respond to someone that has their preachy pants on, but a kind and sensitive gesture—like a sandwich or a bowl of hot soup—can show the love of God like nothing else can.

With gratitude, I think about how my grandmother's mission field was not only her community but her family too! I remember sleeping over at her house and her picking me out of all the grandkids to sneak back into her room in the morning and

drink coffee with her in her bed. Her bed was layered with cozy quilts and chenille blankets. Oh, the scent of that room was a mixture of floral perfumes, baby powder, and minty skin cream. The scents of a queen.

I would prop up the fluffy pillows to a sitting position while she would load up her special tray with coffee and sweet love and put it in the perfect spot between us on the bed. She would pour just a tiny bit of coffee in the bottom of my mug and then fill the rest up with milk and sugar. I even had a special spoon to stir it between my sips. We talked about life lessons, the day ahead, and anything else we wanted to share. Clearly, I was her favorite. (Years later, I found out she did this with all her grandkids, and of course, each of us thought we were her favorite.)

It's wonderful to send money to organizations that help educate and feed children or dig wells for drinking water in a third-world country. Just don't forget to also look around right where you are. Sometimes you can make the most powerful impact in your hometown, just like Nonnie did. You could leave a new sleeping bag for the homeless individual behind the fire station or pack your teens in the car and drive around and pass out fast-food gift cards to individuals in need on the street corners.

By volunteering at the food pantry or a local career and housing organization, you can help individuals get back to work and find affordable housing. Consider who in your neighborhood might need a bag of groceries, a ride to the store, or someone to sit and have coffee with them to listen to their family stories. There are many ways to shine God's light and plant seeds of hope for a better future.

The Chest of Treasures

Cherishing your heritage and family traditions can bring a sense of pride and connectedness in these disconnected times. I'm a firm believer that heirloom crystal or china should be used regularly if you are lucky enough to be entrusted with such a gift. It's time to pull these treasures out of the cabinet, wash them, and enjoy them with your loved ones.

When Grandma Stenner died, her parents' antique bench was passed down to our family. It is placed center stage in our family room. Many muddy boots have been taken off and dinner guests pulled up to the table while sitting on this treasure. We use and enjoy it and occasionally tell a story about Virginia, passing on her memories to the next generation.

Our barn is full of tackle boxes, rusted garden shovels, and basic tools that we use regularly while they remind us of the special person that passed them down to us. Gramps's helmet from the war was first given to CJ to play with as a young child and then passed on to our boys. It wasn't gathering dust on a shelf; it was lovingly put on the head of a nine-year-old boy to play with as he began to ask about our country's history.

Heritage and traditions do not have to be physical objects but can be a young family or friends making new memories together. I can recall taking a simple walk through the woods with my father and grandpa as they both helped me find huge and colorful fall leaves on a waterside trail at Line Creek Park in our hometown. My dad used every opportunity possible to instill in me worldly common sense and, more importantly, his faith and awe of God's love and creation. Every time I see a massive, brilliant orange maple leaf in the fall, I smile. It's making the time for those little moments that can ground us.

The month before I was married, my mama sat me down at her kitchen table and went through her recipe box. The gift of her favorite mealtime instructions was

The grace-filled life shapes meaningful memories and a legacy of grit, grace, and gratitude.

priceless. They weren't pinned on Pinterest but handwritten, complete with vanilla and batter stains. Over the years, as we've made the dishes, I've savored every bite of those scrumptious recipes entrusted to the next generation. Flipping through the recipes and pages of old photo albums together, our children need to hear the stories of those that forged the path ahead of them. Storytelling is a treasured art we are trying to preserve.

One of my favorite pieces, my mom's soup tureen, is always on display in the kitchen and occasionally filled to the rim for a simple soup and salad brunch. Using these special pieces to serve a main course or as a flower vase for favorite blooms makes a simple gathering memorable. These are the family heirlooms and traditions I treasure most and will enjoy passing along to the next generations.

Learning about your history and family traditions might help you recognize traits you share with your ancestors and give you that needed encouragement to pursue a lifelong dream, such as starting your own homestead. Grit, imagination, resourcefulness, and the senses of delight and wonder are qualities of those who desire this rich life.

Share Your Story of Simple Beginnings

God has a purpose for your life and family. If I was the betting type, I would bet that he's already laid that on your heart. On our honeymoon many years ago, we were in a shop that was handing out water due to the heatwave. As we left the store and shared sips from the plastic water bottle, we noticed that there was a scripture sticker on it. It read, "We know that in all things God works for the good of those who love him, who have been called according to his purpose" (Romans 8:28).

As two young and silly kids in love, we claimed it for our life verse as we started out this adventure of marriage together. We honestly didn't think much of it at the time. Through all the years and struggles of newborn babies in the hospital, surgeries, sick parents, job changes, and more, we've come back to this promise verse over and over.

I don't know much, but I do know that God is faithful. He has answered our prayers, and when the answer was no, years later it was clear why. God is there every step of the way, working things out for us and for you. In all things, God works for the good of those that love him. We have been called according to his purpose.

It's important to share our lineage, history, and traditions, but we will also be passing down the stories of God's faithfulness to our family. It's like a beautiful time line of him showing up in our lives. Share your faith journey with your littles. If certain individuals or favorite authors have inspired your faith, share their names and quotes with your loved ones to spark the curiosity to research their stories.

We named our goats after some amazing pillars of faith that have pointed us back to God's Word during difficult times in our family. A.W. Tozer, C.S. Lewis, and Charles Spurgeon are the members of this goat gang. Who knows, we may even add a goat named Oswald Chambers someday.

History Starts Today

There are many that might not know their family lineage or have stories of their grandparents' pasts. If this is you, don't lose heart. History making is happening right now. The traditions you start will create a known history and the story of your homestead journey, whether it's from your high-rise balcony or a 40-acre ranch. It's easy to strengthen a heritage for your loved ones to remember. Start with one new tradition per season and watch how your shared legacy grows. Here are some memorable ideas:

- Choose a favorite recipe that you will continue to enjoy with your family or friends at a certain holiday or time of year. One of our sons always wants a creamy cheesecake for his birthday dessert, so cheesecake it is!

- Build or find a treasured piece together. This could be a simple wooden bench or birdhouse. If you are not the crafty type, head to the thrift or antique store together and pick out a serving platter or special piece to incorporate into your gatherings. It could be beautiful and ornate or better yet, comical and obnoxious to bring the giggles out.

- Schedule an outing that you look forward to every year. We enjoy a short drive north to a farm and apple orchard each fall to pet their precious animals, pick pumpkins, and devour fresh hot apple fritters.

- Plant something together, whether that's a salsa container garden, a fruit tree, or a flowering bush. This will cultivate the soil and your soul. A stroll outside with your loved ones to check on your plants brings continuous bonding and bounty for years to come.

Building a foundation and new traditions can be a common thread in your family's tapestry. Schedule these precious times, share the stories of when God showed up for your family, laugh, and enjoy your people while making memories that last a lifetime.

Homesteaders are trading material possessions for veggie garden beds and coops full of chickens. As our families are saying goodbye to the busy hustle and seeking out a life of intention and purpose, we fully understand that it is less about the amount of space one has and more about the mindset. It's not about achievement but all about tending to what matters for our loved ones and forming a new way of

living that becomes a legacy. We're picking up those old family recipes, cultivating the gardens, and spending more time on the front porch with those we love.

After 20 years on this small farm, we still don't have our act together, but we sure have come a long way. My hope is you will come alongside the Grace-Filled Homestead, where we embrace the simple beauty in our imperfections, live off the land, and grow a deeper relationship with our Creator. Let's get dirty and grow some deep roots.

TIRE SWING

Nothing says farm scene like an old-fashioned tire swing. They are economical and easy, and this simple addition will give the young and old hours of fun and treasured memories.

SUPPLIES
— Old tire
— 15-foot rope, 1 inch in diameter

DIRECTIONS

1. Location, location, location. First determine which hardwood tree is best for this swing, and then thoughtfully pick a large, well-placed branch. A rule of thumb is that it should be 8 feet high and at least 6 inches thick.

2. Clean the old tire thoroughly. Then scrub it again. There is nothing worse than an Easter dress ruined from a dirty tire swing. Been there, done that.

3. Drill 3 holes in what will be the bottom of the tire once it is hung to allow the rainwater to drain.

4. Secure the rope to the limb and the tire using a simple knot. To avoid fraying, you can wrap the ends with duct tape or burn them.

5. Hang so the tire is at least a foot off the ground. Don't go too high, or the little ones won't be able to reach it.

Enjoy the giggles as you soar toward the sky.

HEIRLOOM CAPRESE SALAD

At the Grace-Filled Homestead, we can't get enough cheese. Fresh mozzarella is one of our favorites. Pair it with large heirloom tomatoes for a true masterpiece. This dish is a staple at our house, served as an appetizer, side dish, or even a special snack. The platter is usually cleared empty in less than two minutes.

INGREDIENTS

½ cup balsamic vinegar
2 tsp. honey
4 large heirloom tomatoes
1 lb. fresh mozzarella
24 fresh basil leaves
Extra virgin olive oil for drizzling
Course ground salt and pepper to taste
Pinch of chili powder

DIRECTIONS

In a saucepan, whisk together the balsamic vinegar and honey. Simmer over medium heat for 2 minutes. Reduce the heat and simmer for approximately 8 minutes. Don't overcook—it will thicken when cooled. Slice the tomatoes and mozzarella into ¼-inch-thick slices.

Layer alternating slices of tomatoes and mozzarella on a large platter. Add whole fresh basil leaves to the top. Drizzle extra virgin olive oil and the cooled balsamic reduction on top. Sprinkle a pinch of chili powder over the dish. Season with salt and pepper to taste.

A Path to Homestead Happiness

Chase your dreams over, under, or through that fence. Persevere.

Simple beauty lies within our imperfections. Embrace them.

Intentional living brings joy. Laser focus on what's important.

Simplicity is sweet. Limit the possessions.

Hard work is holy work. No job is beneath you.

Don't follow the crowd. Be your unique self.

People are more important than things. Take care of your tribe.

Heritage is worth preserving. New is not always better.

Cultivate the soil and your soul. Replenish both often.

Take a stand. Be bold with kindness. It's a lost art.

Time is more important than money. Live with open hands.

Grace, grit, and gratitude daily. God's truths over everything.

Acknowledgments

Sweet Baby Jesus—thank you for showing me your glory, sending your presence, and letting me see your face. What an honor it is to be one of your miracles. Your *grace* is everything to me, and I will spend my life telling of your goodness.

CJ—thank you for being the most selfless person I've ever known. You are my soul mate and the keeper of my heart and our bucket list of adventures. Your love for God, family, and community shines through every decision you make. You are the love of my life.

Kiddos—thank you for cheering me on and having more wisdom, wit, and integrity than 99 percent of adults. I am beyond honored to be your mom and love you more than life. Continue to be bold and shine God's brilliant light into the world.

Mom and Dad—thank you for your love, support, and modeling of God's beautiful grace. I appreciate you living out Christ's love behind the scenes when the outside world couldn't see. I am blessed to be your daughter.

Dee, close family, and friends—thank you for your endless support, Swiss cake rolls, and prayers this past year. What a beautiful community we have.

Tawny and Jenni at Illuminate Literary—thank you for taking a risk on me, championing my message, and giving your wisdom and guidance every step of the way. You are amazing.

Ruth, Hope, Heather, and the Harvest House Publishers team—thank you for your friendship, insight, and vision for this book. Your encouragement, endless hours of work, and Christlike actions were visible in every single interaction. You are the real deal, and I truly appreciate you.

About the Author

Lana Stenner is an author, college professor, and backyard farmer. Twenty years ago, Lana and her husband, CJ, decided to ditch their fast-paced hustle for the simple life. They found a small farm on the edge of town, moved their four little children into a 100-year-old fixer-upper, and began to focus on God, goats, and gardens at the Grace-Filled Homestead.

Follow Lana's fun barnyard animal videos on Instagram and TikTok and draw inspiration from her recipes and DIY blog at lanastenner.com. There, you'll also discover the Backyard Farm Academy classes and the *Grace-Filled Grit* podcast. Lana is grateful for God's grace and uses her time helping others strengthen their faith, family, and farm.

If you are interested in Lana's free resources on faith, family, and the farm, you can find them online at www.lanastenner.com\freebies. There you will find her free *Backyard Farm Garden Planner, One Year Bible Reading Plan*, recipe guides, and much more.

Connect with Lana
www.lanastenner.com
IG and FB @lanastenner
Pinterest @lanastennerhomestead
TikTok @lanastennerandgoatgang

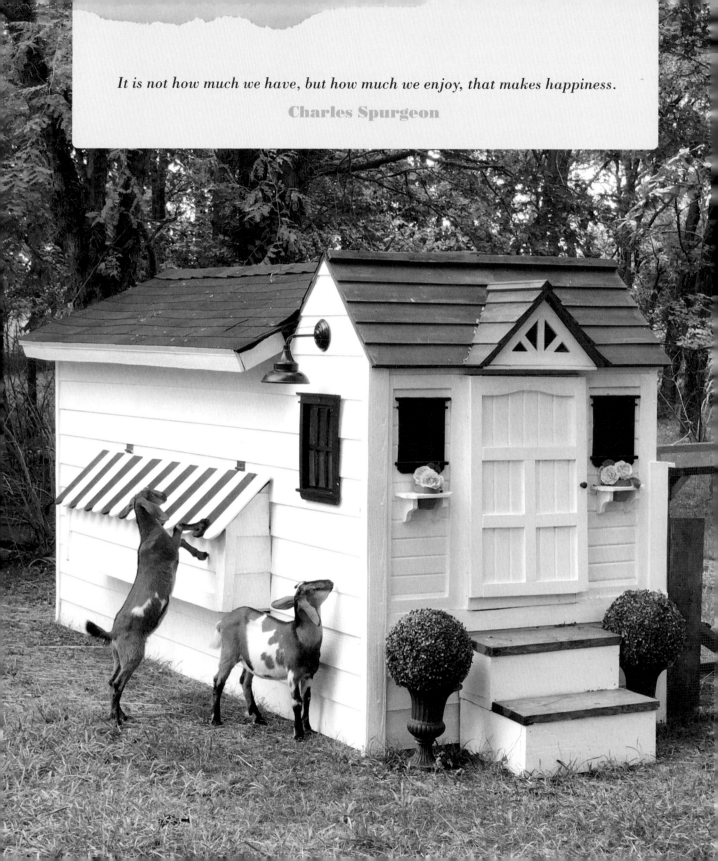

It is not how much we have, but how much we enjoy, that makes happiness.

Charles Spurgeon